Working with
Asperger
Syndrome
in the Classroom

of related interest

Asperger Syndrome in the Inclusive Classroom
Advice and Strategies for Teachers
Stacey W. Betts, Dion E. Betts and Lisa N. Gerber-Eckard
Foreword by Peter Riffle
ISBN 978 1 84310 840 5

Asperger Syndrome – What Teachers Need to Know
Matt Winter
ISBN 978 1 84310 143 7
Written for Cloud 9 Children's Foundation

Count Me In!
Ideas for Actively Engaging Students
in Inclusive Classrooms
Richard Rose and Michael Shevlin
Foreword by Paul Cooper
ISBN 978 1 84310 955 6

Common SENse for the Inclusive Classroom
How Teachers Can Maximise Existing Skills
to Support Special Educational Needs
Richard Hanks
ISBN 978 1 84905 057 9

Addressing the Challenging Behavior of
Children with High-Functioning Autism/
Asperger Syndrome in the Classroom
A Guide for Teachers and Parents
Rebecca A. Moyes
ISBN 978 1 84310 719 4

No Fighting, No Biting, No Screaming
How to Make Behaving Positively Possible for People
with Autism and Other Developmental Disabilities
Bo Hejlskov Elvén
ISBN 978 1 84905 126 2

The Complete Guide to Asperger's Syndrome
Tony Attwood
ISBN 978 1 84310 495 7 hardback
ISBN 978 1 84310 669 2 paperback

Working with
Asperger
Syndrome
in the Classroom

An Insider's Guide

Gill D. Ansell

Jessica Kingsley *Publishers*
London and Philadelphia

First published in 2011
by Jessica Kingsley Publishers
116 Pentonville Road
London N1 9JB, UK
and
400 Market Street, Suite 400
Philadelphia, PA 19106, USA

www.jkp.com

Copyright © Gill D. Ansell 2011
Printed digitally since 2012

Library of Congress Cataloging in Publication Data
Ansell, Gill D.
 Working with Asperger syndrome in the classroom : an insider's guide /
Gill D. Ansell.
   p. cm.
 Includes index.
 ISBN 978-1-84905-156-9 (alk. paper)
 1. Autistic children--Education. 2. Asperger's syndrome. I. Title.
 LC4717.A57 2011
 371.94--dc22
                         2010025673

British Library Cataloguing in Publication Data
A CIP catalogue record for this book is available from the British Library

Contents

Preface

Having recently visited France, and my French being far from fluent, I realised, yet again, how difficult it is to try communicating with people who don't understand what is being said or expected of them. Fortunately, I had my little magic book (*le livre de magie*) in the guise of an English/French, French/English dictionary to help me. But what about those children with Autistic Spectrum Disorders (ASDs) who have difficulty understanding any language, even the language of the country they live in? What help is there for them in mainstream education? Some of them get extra support from education staff, but so little appears to be known, in the mainstream sector, of strategies and ways to interact appropriately with these children. I have realised that it is more important than ever for me to write a book that aims to help those teaching assistants and teachers working with children with Asperger syndrome, to find and help develop ways which will enable these students to understand the world around them a bit better so that they are more able to function appropriately in school, with peers and in society in general. After all, what is the use of knowledge if it is not shared in a good way? I have been lucky enough to have some experience of working with children with ASDs and have seen successful outcomes for children on the autistic spectrum, where perhaps others feared there was none. A little knowledge can go a long way, if used in the right way, and I would like to share with you some of the strategies I have put into practice and used over the past 14 years.

Also, I have included some small snippets in the book (see Chapter 32) because I believe these help us to understand how children with ASDs behave. They are a useful tool, quick to read and easy for us to process. I have been given books to read which have loads of technical jargon in and, to be honest, I get lost after a few pages and although they may well contain useful information, I do not have the time, or patience, to read further.

I hadn't sought to work with children with Asperger syndrome. It was just, sort of, thrust upon me. I'd known from when I had been working with children in a pre-school setting that I got most of my job satisfaction from working with children with special needs and it progressed from there. The children with challenging behaviour gave me a challenge and I liked that.

However, before I start, I think it is important that you know something about me so maybe you can understand a little of why I feel I can offer some advice to you.

So, this is me: after leaving school and doing several different jobs, including various hotel jobs, farm work, and a few years in the army, I had my own children. While they were young and able to attend pre-school, I worked as a pre-school supervisor and later, in another pre-school, as a deputy supervisor. Whilst being the deputy supervisor of a pre-school, I spent a lot of time with a student who exhibited challenging behaviour: spitting milk in my face at snack time, flitting from activity to activity like a whirling dervish, and dragging other children off one of the two go-carts because he wanted it! (The go-carts were almost identical, same colour, same size, except one had a different bumper.) This child also liked having the same rhyming story read time and again and I was usually the one who read and reread it to him each morning. I knew the words to *No, No, Charlie Rascal* inside out, but fortunately, over time, I have forgotten them. When I say time and again, I don't mean several times a week, I mean several times each morning, cover to cover, over and over again. No matter how hard I tried to change the storybook, he wouldn't settle until I'd read him this story. At home time, he'd hide under the piano at the end of the church hall and his mum had to persuade him to come out. We had someone from the medical profession come out to visit him and autism was mentioned, but we (playgroup staff) knew nothing about this condition or what to do to help him before he moved on to infant school, which he was due to do a few weeks after the assessment. Although I enjoyed working with all the children, I found myself more interested in working with the children who had special needs and/or behavioural problems. I decided that this was an area I was more interested in. So, as my own children got older, I made the decision to broaden my horizons and try working solely with children with special needs.

I then found the nearest special school and rang them up and asked for a visit. It catered for junior school aged children with autism and I began working, as one of two special support assistants, in one of the classrooms of six children, shortly afterwards.

I was really enjoying this new challenge and learning about the condition, through experience and reading informative (though easy to understand) books about autism, but then the school moved premises and the distance for me to travel each day was too far as I still had two young children myself. So, I transferred to another local school, this time catering for junior and secondary school aged children with Asperger syndrome. It was a big change for me, in such a short space of time, as I had gone from working with children aged two and a half to working with Year 10 students in four months. I was not sure of how capable I would be in my new role, working as a special support assistant for 14 and 15-year-olds. I was out of my comfort zone but determined to do well and get as much experience as I could with such an interesting condition. I was lucky because the training I received at this school was ideal – up to date, informative and relevant – and the staff I worked alongside were extremely helpful and supportive.

After working at this school for a while, I learned about the ability to 'think outside the box'. This is where you are able to think outside the normal way of thinking, coming up with ideas that may not have been tried before but that may have a chance of working if you just have the courage to give them a go. For example, a child is unable to enter the maths classroom for some unknown reason. The average way of thinking would be 'Well, all the others can go into the room without a problem so there's no reason why he can't. Let's keep bringing him along and I'm sure he'll come in sooner or later.' In the meantime, the child, who has difficulty with language skills and expressing himself anyway, not only misses out on maths lessons, but gets more anxious about going to the room each time as well. This alone can cause negative behaviours and heighten anxiety levels, something children with ASDs are susceptible to.

By thinking outside the box, you are able to come up with more, maybe unusual ideas of why the child cannot enter the room. For instance, it could be that the teacher has a particular aroma or scent and the child does not like this smell. It could be that the child had a bad experience in a maths class before he came to your school and this upsets him and reminds him. It could be that someone has great expectations about his maths capabilities and he is afraid of not living up to them. Then, of course, are the ways to tackle it. Is the child over-sensitive to smells? Is he capable of doing the maths work set? Could he do the work in another room, perhaps by moving a table outside the main classroom? Could the teacher try having a re-laxed and informal chat with the child in a neutral place at some time? This could give the child the chance to see the teacher in a non-threatening environment and to have a casual chat, maybe finding some things out about each other, for example that they both support the same foot-ball team or share a similar hobby. If none of these ideas work, keep thinking and don't give up. If everyone went along with the norm of what everyone else believes and thinks, then nothing new would ever be invented. For me, this is all part of the challenge – where others have been unable to make a positive change to a negative behaviour, I want to find one, not to prove others wrong but because I feel that the child has to be given every opportunity to function and be happy in their day-to-day life.

I stayed with this school for five years and started to feel I was no longer making a difference to the children I was working with, so I decided to leave and have a complete break from working with children – I went to work at a small jam factory! However, after one month, I saw an advert for a teaching assistant (TA) to work afternoons with a child with Asperger syndrome in a local mainstream school, preferably with some knowledge of Asperger syndrome. So, I ended up in a junior mainstream school for three years, initially working one to one with a child with Asperger syndrome and challenging behaviour, though I soon started working with more groups of children with learning difficulties and taking Emotional Literacy sessions for small groups of children with difficulties in making friends and functioning in the classroom setting.

After some success with the child with Asperger syndrome, he was able to manage his behaviour better in the school day, and it was then suggested by the educational psychologist for our school, that maybe other teaching staff from local schools could come to visit us and we could tell them what we had achieved and how we had achieved it. At this point, I must make it clear that I did not achieve this success alone – it was done with teamwork, hard work, determination and the child wanting to achieve. The educational psychologist, Sue, had encountered many other mainstream schools in her catchment area that were having similar problems to us but some had not yet achieved much success.

Throughout the past 11 years, I have worked with children who have sworn, punched, kicked, spat, pinched, bitten, thrown things and much more but I can honestly say it hasn't got to me. I have always made a point of seeing the positives of every situation, even when it has been very difficult to do so at the time and I think it is important to be able to do this. I can remember being very cross about having a painful knee ligament injury caused by a child who fell to his knees as I was taking him from class (using a recognised restraint used by many schools) for behaviour reasons. At first I was cross at him (although I was mindful not to let him know this), and my thoughts were that if he hadn't been silly and dropped to his knees, then I wouldn't be sitting with my leg elevated watching daytime television for the next four weeks!

However, as I sat at home with my leg up, a pair of crutches close by, I thought through the incident from the antecedent to the actual time I felt my knee crack. Now I was more relaxed I was able to analyse more honestly and see past my painful leg. The incident occurred because the teacher was, albeit inadvertently, winding this student up, making a point of telling him he was ignoring him and then laughing (perhaps nervously, as he was quite a new teacher) as the boy got more agitated. The child was then unable to control his frustration and I ended up taking him from class and getting myself injured. So really, it was not the boy's fault. This teacher could have handled the situation differently, and the outcome of this incident could have been much more positive. This can be the case for so many incidents when you actually sit back and analyse exactly what led up to it. The important thing is that we learn from our own, and our colleagues', mistakes and try to ensure the same things don't happen again.

Only by analysing ourselves, and the part we, as adults, play in children's challenging behaviours, can we remain positive and move forward for a new day, *every* day, with the child. You will need to accept that you *will* make mistakes. It is all part of our learning to be better at the jobs we do, and thinking again on a positive note, we will probably remember something better if we made a mistake with it the first time. Just pick yourself up, dust yourself down and get back to it. You will no doubt make more mistakes in your lifetime, but you will also do a lot of learning.

From when I was quite young, I have always had the belief that if someone tells me I can't do something, I will find a way to prove them wrong. This idea has served me well with the challenges I have had in my working career so far and I firmly believe that sometimes, when the usual methods of achieving the goal seem unobtainable, I have to find other ways of achieving it (otherwise known as thinking outside the box). This is something that can be achieved by yourself or by talking with your peers, pooling ideas and deciding on the best way forward.

Introduction

Working with Asperger Minds

▬ ▬ ▬ ▬ ▬ ▬ ▬ ▬ ▬ ▬ ▬ ▬ ▬

I wrote this book because I felt there was something missing on the bookshelves: a book which would be useful for teaching assistants (TAs), teachers new to working with children with a diagnosis of Asperger syndrome (AS), pre-school workers, or anyone working or living with someone with AS. It is not meant as a long, in-depth book about AS – I will leave that to the experts. That's not to say I'm not an expert, because when you have worked intensely with children with an Autistic Spectrum Disorder (ASD), I think you become an expert on the condition merely through the process, not through research. My book is meant as a book of little ideas that could make big, positive changes to a child in mainstream education. If you are a parent or carer of a child with AS, there could well be some ideas here that could help your child at home, or at their school. It is meant to show that these are ideas that can work, as I have tried them all and found that they can. It is also meant as a guide, not a book that is guaranteed to work for every child, as it won't do that. It is meant to give you some ideas to get you started, and ideas that you could adapt to suit your needs, your school's needs and the child's needs (not necessarily in that order!).

I was prepared to work hard to get results and I understand that sometimes we need to think outside the box. I am just an ordinary, hard-working mother, trying to make ends meet, but I am also confident that methods I used in classrooms have worked and helped children with AS understand the world a little better. In short, I am your typical TA, whether mainstream or special needs.

I worked, as a special support assistant and TA, with children with AS, for about 11 years and, I have to say, every child has been different. Currently I am working as an ASD adviser for an advisory and support group.

I think it is important to remember at this point that AS is a syndrome, and the definition of a syndrome is: *a group of signs and symptoms that together are characteristic or indicative of a specific disease or disorder.* That means that to have a diagnosis of AS, a person must meet certain criteria in their behaviours but not necessarily *all* the criteria. So, forget any hearsay about people with AS not understanding sarcasm, because some do. Forget also that people with AS don't show empathy, because some do. And forget that people with AS can't read body language, because again, some do. Remember to treat each child with AS as an individual, because they are. Try also to understand their way of thinking, as it can be very logical. After all, if we all thought the same way, and all had the same likes and dislikes, how boring would that be?

Information in this book is based on strategies and resources that I have personally used successfully in assisting children with AS to manage inappropriate classroom behaviour and which have also, over time, helped them manage their own behaviour in other situations outside school. Many of the strategies I write about are not necessarily solely for use with children with an ASD though, as many of the strategies can be used for other children where deemed appropriate. Some of the strategies are ones I have adapted myself from experience of other strategies, whilst others are ones I have learnt from reading some of the valuable resources now available on the market. Where necessary, I have named the resources I have used.

An important point concerning any information is that you take what is relevant to you, use it and adapt it for your own needs and that of the child you are working with.

I must add that the success of these strategies would not have been possible without support from my fellow TAs, headteachers, teachers, educational psychologists and the parents of the children. Therefore, it is my belief that the following strategies will be much more effective if all-round support is available to you and your ideas.

The support needed is to back up what you are doing but also to be there when you try a new strategy for the first time and it doesn't go exactly to plan. Remember to take constructive criticism as a positive thing and learn from it. You also need to have some hardy staff who are brave enough to go against the grain and allow a child to be removed from lessons for behaviour management or even to complete their work outside the main classroom. In the UK, where so much emphasis is put on national results and positioning in league tables, it is often the children with special educational needs who get forgotten. This should not be allowed to happen. *All* children deserve an equal chance to achieve their full potential (see *Every Child Matters*, a government programme of change to improve outcomes for all children and young people). In fact, most schools have a Vision Statement, which includes something similar about helping all children achieve their full potential. If this is true of your school, then you can take pride in playing your part to help them to achieve this.

Some education staff may be reluctant to allow a child time out of the main classroom because it's not what is supposed to happen in mainstream education. What we should be asking ourselves is this: what is the point of having a disruptive child in the classroom for four years if they are going to disrupt the learning of 20 or 30 or so other children and not be able to access the curriculum themselves either? Surely it is better that they have several months, if required, out on their own with one-to-one, or small group support and are then able to be gradually re-integrated into the classroom with others. That way, every child has the opportunity to succeed, and the disruption of the whole class is limited. Not only is this a good way for all the children to be able to access the curriculum, in their own way, but it is an excellent use of the TA. It is also about differentiation, which *all* educators should be doing for *all* children anyway, whether the child is behind academically, has a special need, or is very gifted and talented. It is part of *Every Child Matters*, because actually, every child does matter. The policy document states that the aim of the *Every Child Matters* programme is to give all children the support they need to:

- be healthy

- stay safe

- enjoy and achieve

- make a positive contribution

- achieve economic well-being.[1]

---

1   Department for Children, Schools and Families (2009) *Aims and Outcomes.* Available at www.dcsf.gov.uk/everychildmatters/about/aims/aims, accessed on 16 August 2010.

Although the roles of both the TA and the teacher are, in reality, very different, they are both striving for the same outcome for the children in their care – to enable them to achieve in the best way that they can. For children to have any chance of achieving their full potential, teachers and TAs must work closely together as a team, with each having an understanding of the other's roles and responsibilities. The teacher's role is to take overall responsibility for the education of the child, whereas the TA's role is to help the teacher achieve that. Both needs the other, and for that there needs to be a mutual respect for each other's roles. Whereas the teacher has to teach a *whole* class, the TA is able to work outside the classroom with one child or a small group of children, normally under the guidance of the teacher. This is because the role of the TA has changed considerably over the last few years. They are no longer the 'mother-helpers' they once were, but are now trained to help their teacher deliver the curriculum more effectively and have a better understanding of curriculum matters as well as child development.

When the teacher and TA work as part of a team this can benefit the children and help them feel that things in class are consistent, when perhaps in other areas of their lives, there is nothing but inconsistency. How confusing would it be for them if the TA and teacher both had very different ideas and both voiced them and never seemed to agree on anything? If you are a teacher, take a moment to imagine how your life in the classroom would be without your TA, or any stand-in support, to help with your children, resources and display boards, for a week. If you are a TA, take a moment to think about how your life would be without the teacher in your class for a week, if you were solely in charge of all the children and responsible for their education and behaviours. Perhaps then, you will see that both needs the other to enable the classroom, and all that goes on in it, to function most effectively.

The support from colleagues is also needed when you decide you want to try something never tried in your school before. I was lucky in that one headteacher and senior TA were always keen for me to suggest new things and try them out. Fortunately, with this support, I was able to work closely with a child (who had been permanently excluded from a previous mainstream school before they arrived with us).

When this child first started at the school in Year 3, aged seven, she only attended in the mornings with one-to-one support and had daily tantrums and aggressive outbursts. After a term she attended for the afternoons (which is why I was initially employed) as well but went home every lunch hour because of her behaviour and the way it impacted on her peers. However, after several years of consistent teamwork, she was able to attend all day, including lunches, and successfully managed to attend school residential trips with no major incidents. If ever there was a way to measure success, this is surely it.

If you have a child with AS and/or who has challenging behaviours coming to your school, be excited at all that you can learn from him or her, and all the new challenges that will face you and your colleagues. Look forward to the success you and your team can achieve when working together. It can seem a daunting time, but you are not alone, you have a team who can work through this together with you and support you when you need it. It can also be a new learning curve for you, if you have not encountered a challenge like this before.

Note: For ease of reference I have alternated the use of male and female pronouns for each chapter.

Part I

WHAT IS ASPERGER SYNDROME?

Chapter 1

Autistic Spectrum Disorders

There are many books out there about Autistic Spectrum Disorder (ASD), autism, Asperger syndrome (AS) and high-functioning autism. I will briefly explain what an ASD is. For more in-depth explanations I suggest you visit your local bookshop or library.

Autism was a word I'd heard of before but knew very little about. The first book I was advised to read on the subject was *Autism: The Facts* by Simon Baron-Cohen and Patrick Bolton[2] and it really was a book which explained autism to me in an easy and understandable way. It was my first insight into understanding something of the condition and a book I would recommend. After reading it, and after briefly working with children with autism, I developed a strong interest in the condition.

People with ASDs have difficulties in three main areas of their lives: communication, socialisation and inflexibility of thought. This is known as the Triad of Impairment.

Communication is something most of us take for granted. We learn to communicate from a very young age, learning from our parents how to interact with each

---

2   Baron-Cohen, S. and Bolton, P. (1993) *Autism: The Facts*. Oxford: Oxford University Press.

other, that if we say something to someone, the other person is likely to respond. When the majority of us communicate with each other, we also use body language as a way to express ourselves – raised eyebrows, screwed-up noses, lip curls, hand waves and various hand movements, body stance – and we can read more into what a person is trying to say with these gestures. However, a person with an ASD will not necessarily notice these visual cues or understand their meanings and will therefore not get the full meaning of what, or how, something has been said. Tone of voice is also something which is misunderstood and people with an ASD often have to be taught about tone of voice and what different tones could mean, both when used by them and by others. Socialisation is also something we learn to do at a young age, when we visit relatives and friends, start school and go to parties and make friendships. Turn taking plays a big part in both of these skills. However, a child with an ASD will not understand the way either of these works. He won't pick up on social cues, for example, that we take it in turns to talk, known as a conversation, and that it is thought to be rude not to give eye contact when you are being spoken to, that we don't interrupt and monopolise the conversation with a special interest (for example talking non-stop about trains and how they work). He won't understand that someone may be showing signs of being bored with his constant talk of computers – arms folded, raised eyeballs looking to the sky, fidgeting, foot tapping – and may well continue to talk for a long time before the other person walks off, particularly if it is children talking to children as they may well have not learned yet that this is not the socially acceptable thing to do. They may well have to be taught this in a very clear way.

Inflexibility of thought is something many of us have but we can be swayed with simple argument – for example, someone else has used the cup I always like at coffee break, but I can reason with myself that it is not life threatening to me if I don't use it today. However, a person with an ASD could well see it as the one thing that upsets the rest of his day. He always uses a particular cup and therefore he can't have his morning drink because he doesn't have that cup to put it in and he may well think that the person using the cup knows he wanted that cup but used it anyway. This could then upset his ability to think, as this incident, although minor to most of us, will over-ride his thought process and make him unable to think clearly. If he knows he always uses that cup, then he may well believe everyone else should know he always uses that cup, making him feel rejected because someone has used it knowing it would upset him. This brings me to 'theory of mind'. Again, there are many books around which talk in great depth about this subject but I will just give a brief explanation.

A little about theory of mind

In simple terms, the theory of mind is where we can think we know what another person may be thinking or feeling by reading his body language, his facial expressions and his eyes. We can guess what his next move may be, what he intends to do next given the information he has just received, or given his previous behaviours. Theory of mind is not a psychological theory, it is something that the majority of people develop in order to understand the minds of other people. It is known as a theory because it is not a fact, because we cannot actually know for certain how another's mind is thinking, unless that person tells us. Most of us will use our theory of mind daily, without realising it – that driver wasn't happy with me because she looked angry when I took the last parking space; the assistant in the cafe was pleased with me because I had the correct money and they were probably short of change in the till; the lady was upset with me because my trolley bumped into hers and even though she smiled at me, her eyes told me she was annoyed. For someone to develop theory of mind, he first has to be aware of his own emotions, desires and self-awareness. However, a child with an ASD may not have developed this theory of mind (a condition often now referred to as mindblindness) and he will therefore find understanding the world around him even more complicated than it already is. Please bear all these things in mind when working with a child with an ASD and try to show him ways to make the world around him less scary by explaining things he finds confusing in a clear way that he can understand. It may take more than once for him to understand but be patient, it is well worth the effort to see a child progress and be happy and know that you played a part in making that happen.

Chapter 2

Understanding Asperger Syndrome

Even in today's society, with all the information available to us, some people have still not heard of AS, and some that have know very little about it. If you are going to be working with a child with this condition, and the staff at your school have limited knowledge about the condition, it may be an idea to invite a parent or parents of a child with AS into your school to give staff a talk about it. It can be very enlightening, because what we read in books about the condition may well be very different from how an individual child actually is. After all, the parent is living with someone with ASD and will no doubt be a fountain of knowledge. They will be able to give you a good insight into the difficulties faced as well as the benefits of it. Knowing how a child reacts at home can also be very informative – bedtime routines, mealtimes, sibling friendships, etc. all give a better understanding of the impact AS can have, not only on an individual child, but also on the whole family. Knowing what the family goes through every day may make you a bit more understanding the next time the parent (of a child with AS) phones up complaining that her child is upset because of something that has happened at school. It could also enhance the parent/ school partnership which is *always* a good thing.

If the child with AS does not know a great deal about AS, it can be a good idea, with parents' permission, to do a series of Behaviour Management sessions covering the topic. After all, if the child has the syndrome, surely it can only benefit her if she understands it, and therefore herself, better. A child I worked with knew she had AS, and that her dad had it too, but she did not realise other people had it as well and when we researched it on the internet, she was amazed, and really focused on reading about them and their difficulties. Suddenly, she knew she was not alone and this had a positive effect on her and her outlook.

The internet is a great place to find out about famous people with AS. I have worked with many students with AS who see Microsoft's Bill Gates (believed to have AS) as a hero. If he can achieve and be as successful as he has been, they see no reason why they can't. It was quite interesting for me too, seeing these stars and realising that they may have AS, and seeing what they can achieve in their adult lives. AS doesn't have to be all doom and gloom and I think many people would not have achieved all they have *without* their AS. When doing this though, you need to be careful about what you are allowing the child to read. Some information can be quite negative and, though it may be good for the child to get more informa- tion on her condition, you need to remember too, that she *is* a child, and too much information can be a dangerous thing. A lot of these children have high anxieties and I am certainly not suggesting you allow them free rein over the internet or access to the many available books, but that you allow them to understand a little more of their condi- tion. I have found information on the internet, printed it off and cut out the parts that I have felt were relevant for them, deliberately omitting parts that were not beneficial for them to read.

I have done scrapbooks with children where they can do their own work on the condition, write their own stories about a child with AS (these can be quite enlightening), write facts they have learned, recap on things that have helped them, or information they have obtained from the internet.

Sometimes I have talked to children with AS about the Triad of Impairment and this alone has been enough to allow them to understand the condition more. Information on this can also be found on the internet or your Special Educational Needs Coordinator (SENCO) may have information. The local library will also be a great source for information on ASDs and associated conditions.

At one school where I worked there were several children with AS, and some that were older than the child I was working with. We (the staff) decided that it might be a good idea to involve one of the older children with AS in some of the younger child's Behaviour Management sessions. So, we asked an older child with AS, who also had behavioural problems, if she would be interested in doing some work with the younger child and she was only too keen. I was amazed at how well they got on and how easy it seemed for them to talk to each other. It was a great success and the two of them discussed how they felt about getting angry and how certain things upset them. The older girl told her that she used to get angry and have disruptive outbursts but that she rarely had them anymore as she could control them much better.

I took a step back and listened to them and I learned a lot from them. It was lovely to see two very anxious girls be so relaxed in each other's company. I believe it gave them both a much needed confidence boost as they both had something in common that few of the other children in their school understood. Plus, my young charge then had a new role model and one of her peers to go to with her problems. At a later date, during another of our one-to-one sessions, I asked her what she would like to achieve by the time she went into Year 6 (age 11). She replied 'I'd like to be as successful as [her role model] is with managing her own behaviours.'

Another idea for helping this kind of peer friendship is to find another school, or even your own school, where the child has email links with another child with AS. Your school educational psychologist may be able to help you set this up. This is something we talked about setting up but never actually got around to doing because the child we were going to do it with left the other school, though I'm certain that, if properly monitored, it could be a successful activity.

Chapter 3

Literal Thinking

I never realised just how strange the English language could be until I spent several years working with children with ASD. Now I find myself getting cross after analysing headlines in papers and thinking how badly they are worded and how they can be misleading. Try reading through a national newspaper and looking at statements and see for yourself how they can be misinterpreted.

The English language is a complicated one on the best of days but now, for me, after spending time with these children, I find myself analysing what *I* say, or write, all the time and thinking about how it could be misinterpreted. Some of the everyday things we say can be quite confusing.

Here are some examples, some of which you may use yourself. If so, always check that the child understands what you have said and ask him what it means in his own words, then, if he has misunderstood, you can tell him what it means.

- Pull your socks up
- Play it by ear
- Keep your hair on
- We take two steps forward and one step back
- Hold your horses
- I'll have that done in two shakes of a lamb's tail
- A leopard cannot change its spots
- A man after my own heart

- A fate worse than death (if a child is terrified of death, then telling him that if he's late for class this will be a fate worse than death could mortify him and throw him into a blind panic.)

- Like a fish out of water

- You're all fingers and thumbs

- We'll have that done before you can say Jack Robinson

- Bob's your uncle

- I've got green fingers

- Blow your own trumpet

- Born with a silver spoon in one's mouth

- Blood is thicker than water

- Come on, shake a leg

- Straight from the horse's mouth

- A bird in the hand is worth two in the bush

- Time flies

By looking at, and analysing, these statements and having the ability to understand them when they are used, it is easy to see how confusing they can be to someone who already has difficulty in understanding language. That is why it is important to try to think about the words you use *before* you actually use them. It could make things go much more smoothly in the classroom.

I was sitting next to a child with AS once when the teacher told the whole class what they were to do next. I asked my charge if he knew what he had to do and he replied that he did, repeating *exactly* what the teacher had said. I then asked him what it meant and he replied, 'I don't know.' If I had not questioned him about his understanding, it might have led to him becoming disruptive. Disruption can be a way of deflecting the fact that the child does not understand what to do. He would rather be thought of as being poorly behaved (which some children find amusing as it stops a lesson) than stupid (the words a child has used when explaining it to me before).

Part II

WORKING WITH AN INDIVIDUAL WITH ASPERGER SYNDROME

Chapter 4

The Beginning

When I first started working in a classroom with students with AS, I wasn't quite sure what I was supposed to do, or what was expected of me. So, I just did what I did best – I was myself. I was firm with the students but helped them when they needed me to, I got to know them and their little ways, I watched how others worked with the students and picked up ideas from them, I learned about the individual children and I read about the condition. Training also played a big part. Fortunately, there was a lot of in-house training available and the school had a budget for training at outside venues, something many schools have but not everyone is aware of – if you think you need training, find out what's available and get yourself booked on a course relevant to your work. Although I have enjoyed and learned from in-house training, I believe training outside the workplace to be invaluable for several reasons. You get to meet people you wouldn't normally work with and can exchange views, ideas and opinions with them. You learn about new ideas and ways to work with students that are fresh for your school and you can then take these ideas back and share them as well as put them into practice.

A good piece of advice is this – once you know you are going to be working with a child with AS, accept the challenge and reap the benefits and the feeling of success when things go right. It's such a great feeling to succeed with a child, especially where others have failed for one reason or another, often for a lack of perseverance or an inability to think outside the box.

An important thing to remember right from the outset is to get to know the child – what she enjoys, what she doesn't like, if she has a special interest (sometimes called an obsession, like dolls or drawing), if she likes or dislikes sport, if she has siblings, or pets, or extended family. All these things can be a way in to the child's life for you to show an interest and make her feel special. If you know a child has a special interest in dinosaurs, when she next comes in to school tell her something about a dinosaur that you know, or ask her about her dinosaur collection. It's much more personal than just saying 'Good morning' (and don't be offended if she doesn't show too much interest in your life interests as being egocentric can be part of their condition). It shows her that you have listened to her and are interested in her as a person and it is a good start to building up a positive relationship with this child. Perhaps you could get her to tell you about her special interest, or build in time during your sessions together to chat about it or do a mini project on it. This can also be used as a good motivator, for example: 'When you have done your maths, then we can do some of your personal project.'

I would also like to add that we should *never* label the child, but label the behaviour. This is something I was taught early on in my role working with children with AS. In my experience, the children that exhibit challenging behaviour have very low self-esteem so, by labelling them as bad it only reinforces what they *think* they already know – that they *are* bad. So, instead of telling them 'I don't like you for doing that' or 'You are a naughty boy/

girl', try saying 'I like you but I don't like that behaviour' or 'I understand that you are upset, but we need to find another way of expressing your anger.' It may seem like a minor thing, but it can make a huge difference.

After all, would you want to work with someone who kept telling you they didn't like 'you'? The child needs to know that she is OK, but that some of her behaviour is not. It takes the emphasis off her and focuses on what behaviour she is exhibiting.

One of the first things I noticed at a mainstream school was that the parent/school relationship was not particularly amicable – neither seemed to respect, or trust, the other. This is quite common. After all, bear in mind what many parents have gone through – their child may have been temporarily or permanently excluded from another school. That alone doesn't sound too bad, but add these other factors: the child probably *wanted* to be at school and it probably caused him or her to feel upset about not being allowed to go; these children are young and need guidance and understanding to make sense of the world around them; the reaction of other parents towards this child and their family; the fight the parents have to go through to get their child statemented (something that helps them to receive the support they need in class to enable them to function); and having to rearrange their own work and lives around everything that gets thrown at them. Is it any wonder that the parents feel upset? As for the school, they should take what information they have on a child, from the records passed to them, but then make their own decision about how this child can be taught. Although a child's behaviour may be really bad in one school, it does not mean that the child is really bad – it merely means that the school staff have not yet found what works for this particular child – and that in itself is part of the challenge.

Keeping that in mind, it is a good idea to invite the parents in to chat to staff about the child's ASD, how it exhibits in this particular child, what they like, what makes them anxious, what sets off negative behaviours, etc. so that everyone can have a better understanding of what to expect. Start with a clean slate – you don't know this child and it would be wrong to judge her on what others have said. This is where you can inform the parent that you are going to try to make things work for their child and that you may need to try several different things before you find something that works. Be honest – if this is the first time you have had a child with such challenging behaviours, tell them. It is better that they know now, and know that you are learning with their child, than believe you know what to do and then find out that you are working in the dark and don't have a clue. This would only add to their distrust of schools and their staff. At least if you are upfront at the start, they know you are going to try your best. After all, a parent knows their child better than anyone – and this is the first phase of the parent/teacher/TA relationship.

Chapter 5

Individual Work Stations

Individual work stations (or bays) are secluded areas which allow the child to have a safe, personal space where he can have time-out and not be in full view of his peers. I think there is a place for these in mainstream schools, particularly in the UK since the introduction of the inclusion policy. The inclusion policy in the UK means that children *with* special needs will be educated alongside children *without* special needs, with some support, in mainstream schools. However, this is not always the best option and a more specialist provision is often needed.

If it means that the child is able to return to the classroom less disruptive, then individual work stations are well worth it. These do not need to be an added expense as they can be made from equipment already in school. I understand that space is limited, but if the choice is another child being injured during a child's aggressive outburst or the majority of the children in class having their lesson interrupted, or finding a small corner big enough to fit a table and a couple of chairs in, then there is no comparison. Find the space, either inside or outside the classroom.

A corner of an area outside, or inside, a classroom provides two sides of a 'bay' and therefore, only a screen is required for one side (if you have a good maintenance man, he may be able to make one up if one is not readily available). The back of a bookcase could even be made use of as the third wall.

The idea of the screen is to give the child a place to focus, without everyone watching them and their behaviours. A TA or teacher can then talk them through an activity without the fear of being watched over by everyone else. Also, other children can be quite a distraction, particularly if the child has not understood the instruction and what is expected of him or her. It is important to understand as well that children with AS often have other conditions alongside it, to a more or lesser degree, such as Attention Deficit Hyperactivity Disorder (ADHD) which will also affect their concentration and behaviours. Displaying negative behaviours can divert the focus of others from their inability to do the work to the fact that the child is behaving badly. Many children would rather have people think they are being naughty than think they cannot do the work that everyone else seems able to do. Besides, admitting in front of everyone that you do not understand what has been said can be a really difficult thing to do. How many of us, as adults, have sat in meetings where something has been said or asked and we haven't put our hand up to ask what is meant because we were afraid that others in the room would think less of us? It is no different for us than it is for the child, but for a child with an ASD, who already has low self-esteem, it is even harder. Also, when one person has been brave enough to put their hand up and questioned what was said, how many of us have breathed a sigh of relief that we were not the only ones who didn't know the answers?

When the child starts to use the bay, it can be a good thing to do some fun activities in it to get him used to it, particularly if he is reluctant to use it in the first place. You could start with some colouring, or decorating it with his own pictures or photos, or looking at a book together. Then, gradually, intersperse work into it, so he gets used to working in his bay. Don't expect things to run smoothly from the start as I'm sure they won't, but persevere as I have said before – it is so worth it in the end.

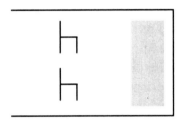

Figure 5.1 A typical work station (bay)

Figure 5.1 shows a typical 'bay', with a table, two chairs and three walls. The chairs are for the child and the TA or teacher. Other children quickly seem to realise that the bay is for a particular child and readily accept, and respect, this as part of the make-up of their school, provided it is shown in a positive way, not as a place for the child to go when he is 'naughty'.

This is an area where the child with AS can go, for their Behaviour Management sessions, or to do his work, or just for time-out or talk time. It is his and, as far as the child with AS is concerned, not somewhere any other child can go unless he or she is invited in for a shared work session or for a reward time. The child may want to decorate the screen with his work, photos of his holiday or special interest or just have them blank. Some children can find too much decoration a distraction which can exacerbate poor behaviour. So, although the bay may look blank and bare to us, it could be exactly what this particular child needs to be calm and to concentrate. Remember, it is *his* area and *his* place to feel safe and relaxed. It could also be a place to display Anger Rules (see p.46).

It is important that he is asked if someone else can go in to use it, though often it is a good idea if it is *not* used by others so that the child with AS realises that it is *his* space whenever *he* needs it. It is an area that needs to be respected so that the child understands the importance of the space. If people respect his space, in time, it is hoped, the child will learn to respect other people's space. It is also important that staff respect the child's bay too. Don't rearrange his pictures, etc. unless you have discussed your reasons for doing so with him. If he doesn't want you to, try to compromise. Sometimes, compromise is a very powerful tool. It also shows the child that you are respecting him and his views.

With one child I was working with, sometimes, while I did Behaviour Management sessions with him outside the main classroom, the teacher would do circle time[3] with the rest of the class and use the time to discuss their concerns about the other child's behaviour, sometimes even explaining aspects of AS. Any issues that came up in their circle time could then be covered by me in future Behaviour Management sessions with him and me

---

3   Circle time is where the whole class sit in a circle, with the teacher included, and discuss topical issues that may concern the children. An example of this could be that bullying has been happening in school. Together, the children explore why this may be happening and what they can do to stop it. Circle time is a safe environment for the children to have their say. If the topical issue is about a child with AS then his parents' permission would need to be sought before discussing this with the whole class.

or with him in the next class circle time. Although some might see this as a breach of the child's confidentiality, it was done with his and his parents' consent and it was beneficial for these other children to gain a better understanding of why he sometimes behaved the way he did. After they were told about what things triggered his behaviours, they were able to help him by avoiding doing things that might upset him, or by being supportive when they saw he was getting anxious.

Chapter 6

Behaviour Management Sessions

These sessions are probably best done by the same person each time, even though two people may be working as the one-to-one assistant for the child (one in the morning and one for afternoons). This is so the delivery is consistent each time and the child knows what to expect.

The work you do in Behaviour Management sessions should be recorded as evidence and will no doubt be looked at during inspections by bodies such as the Office for Standards in Education (OFSTED), though this is nothing to worry about. Your school may have their own recording sheets for recording such sessions, and these may be the same as for recording Emotional Literacy sessions. If there is not a standard recording sheet, suggest one that can be put in place. This is also a good way to record how you think the session went and areas you believe the child needs to continue to work on or move on to next. It also shows other people what you have covered, should you be away for any reason so that someone needs to take over for a short while. It should be regularly checked or overseen by the SENCO or your senior TA to ensure you are doing things correctly.

In order for these children to understand their behaviours and how to change them, they may have to be taught what is acceptable and what is not and why it is or is not.

Remember, their understanding of situations can differ from the majority of us and they may not understand that the way they are behaving is not acceptable. Perhaps their behaviour has never been challenged or explained before or maybe they do not know there are other ways to behave when we are not happy about something. Again, this is something they may need to be shown how to do.

For a child with an ASD this could mean individual sessions involving discussions and role-play, for example, with their allocated TA. These are something that can be done, initially, during the lessons that the child is most disruptive in. Be aware, though, that this may mean that the child is out of class for quite long periods of time each day over a period of several months, but try to remember the bigger picture – that this is an essential activity if you are ever to stand a chance of achieving your overall objective of teaching the child how to manage her own behaviour in order that she can function in the classroom with other children appropriately for longer periods of time.

On occasion, it may be necessary to have impromptu sessions. I have usually done one Behaviour Management session a day though this time has been reduced as the child gets older and more able to manage her behaviour in class. However, if behaviour has been poor during the day, I may take the child to her bay and play a simple board game just so she can redirect her thoughts and regain control. This means we can have a general chat about anything and everything. This may have to happen several times a day – there are no rules about how often you do this. It will depend on what your team decides and the needs of the child.

One of the first things to do in these sessions is to establish the Anger Rules. You can use current school ones, make your own or use some from a book. An example of some Anger Rules are:

> *Never* hurt people.

> *Never* hurt yourself.

> *Never* damage property.

> *Always* tell someone if you are upset.

These may also take into account some of the school's Golden Rules or that is something you could focus on at a later date. Golden Rules are a strategy some schools use to promote positive behaviour. The school sets the rules for students to follow daily and students who follow those rules throughout the week earn something called Golden Time. Golden Time is a reward where the children can do one of various fun activities offered, often on a Friday afternoon, such as model building, drawing, drama, etc. If a child has not followed the Golden Rules all week, she may not earn her full amount of Golden Time but should still earn some of it.

The child may like to make a poster with these rules on to display in her bay or have them minimised to keep in her pocket as a reminder. Again, this is something that can be done during a Behaviour Management session, giving you both the opportunity to chat and get to know each other better. She may want to take a copy home as these rules can apply at home as well. I usually laminate the poster, if it's no bigger than A4 (though if you have an A3 laminator a bigger one could work well too) to show the child that her work is special and can be kept in a good condition for longer. It is also harder to tear up if she is in a destructive 'anti-rules' mood.

It can be a good idea to put in her bay a pot of play-dough and/or a soft, squeezy ball (both very cheap resources) to be held in the hand and squeezed. Show the child how it can be used to help her calm down when she is angry, rather than hitting out at someone. One child I used to work with would make the dough into a person shape then tell me why she was angry with that particular person, before ripping its head off or squashing it in her hands. She was then calmer and able to talk about the problem. We were able to discuss ways to rectify the problem, why it may have happened and how to try to not let the same thing happen again. We also talked about how it was OK to punch the playdough but it is *never* OK to punch another person. At this point we referred to our Anger Rules. It is important for the child to realise that it is OK to have angry feelings but that we have to learn how to deal with them in appropriate ways.

I have told children that when I feel cross I like to squeeze the playdough until it is really flat and they are often keen to prove they can get it flatter than me.

I have found that the child is often reluctant to give you information if you are not prepared to share some yourself. For example, if the child is bad-tempered first thing, on arrival at school, and is reluctant to tell me what has upset her, I might say 'I can see you are upset this morning. I feel like that sometimes. In fact, this morning I slept through my alarm and thought I was going to be late and then I had to rush and couldn't do my hair properly and that made me feel angry with everyone else, even though they hadn't done anything wrong.' Quite often, the child becomes attentive and is keen to hear about why someone else might get upset. She may then be more ready to enter the conversation and say what happened to her that morning that made her so angry. I have felt that, sometimes, the child has felt that she is wrong to feel angry or upset and it is a comfort for her to know that we actually have those feelings too. Remind her often: it's OK to be angry, but it's how we deal with that anger that is important.

I once worked with a child with AS every day for four months before she actually told me she had Asperger's. I told her that I had worked with other children with Asperger Syndrome previously, to which she replied, 'Oh, but I haven't got that, I've just got Asperger's.' When I told her it was all the same thing, it was as if a whole floodgate opened for this child. She seemed amazed that there were other children with AS and that I actually knew something about the condition myself. It does take time to build trust and a bond, but it is a necessity if you are to have a mutual respect with the child. My father always told me 'Patience is a virtue which must be practised' (and I am still practising!).

Whatever you say to the child, make sure you can always follow through as this will help the child believe that she can trust you. For example, if you tell the child that she will have to finish work *during* breaktime if she does not finish it in lesson time, then make sure, beforehand, that this is acceptable in your school, otherwise you make yourself look incompetent to her and your credibility is gone for ever. If you say you will bring something in to show her the next day, make sure you bring it in. Once she knows you can, and will, follow through with what you say you will do, then she can start to trust you. You can help empower the child to understand ways to react to anger that are more appropriate and she will be more willing to try as she will trust you to be right.

Make sure you establish clear boundaries from the start. If a child sees that you keep changing the boundaries then she will lose faith in you. If a child was rude to me, I would correct the behaviour *every* time because it is a life skill to be able to tolerate and respect other people, even if we do not always agree with them. However, I once heard a child being extremely rude to another member of staff and when I was next working with the child, I asked why she was so rude to the other TA. She smirked and replied, 'Because I can be.' I then said, 'But you don't speak to me like that.' To which she replied with a frown, 'No, because you wouldn't let me get away with it!'

All children like to have boundaries, even though they push against them. Boundaries make them feel safe, provided they are enforced, because they know that we can be trusted to help keep them safe. If you have one member of staff not enforcing the boundaries, it can have a huge impact on children's behaviour and the respect for that member of staff is lost. It also causes children to push the boundaries even further, just to see who will win, the member of staff enforcing the boundary or the member of staff not. It is a way to play staff off against each other and for the child this can be a source of power.

How many parents have known children try to play Mum off against Dad (or vice versa) to see who the strongest one is? For the child it can start as a game, but it can have far-reaching consequences. It could show the child that there is conflict between the staff and that is never a good thing. *All* staff should enforce the boundaries (and Golden Rules, which most schools have these days) otherwise the child will see this as a weakness and behaviours can then deteriorate.

Ensure all staff are telling the child/children the same thing, and that some staff aren't allowing children to run through the corridors, while you are constantly telling your one-to-one student to stop running and walk. How fair is that? If this is happening, bring it up at your next staff meeting or with your line manager and see if something can be done to stop the inconsistency.

I have known members of staff who try to be the child's friend but this is not what the child needs. They are children and have other children who can be friends with them. The adults' role is to act as positive role models, and to assist the child in understanding herself and the world around her much more clearly. If a child regularly swears, and is not corrected, then the child is likely to continue, or, worse, 'up the ante'. That means that if she is not getting noticed for her negative behaviour, such as swearing, then the chances are she will do something else that *will* get her noticed, and the attention she needs.

Ignoring the behaviour initially, in fact, does nothing to encourage respect from the child for the adult, and the adult is not helping the child. If the child then goes out in public and swears, I believe the staff member would be equally to blame for not teaching the child that this behaviour is unacceptable.

I understand that confronting a child's negative behaviour can be a bit unnerving, particularly if the child is likely to become aggressive, and it may lead to an incident, but in order for the child to benefit from the support she has then it needs to be done. How else will this child learn that certain behaviours are not acceptable in school or in society in general?

I have worked with children who think it is acceptable to hit out physically at staff but assure me that they would not do it in public. I'm not so sure they have that amount of control when they are upset and so I have talked to them about the consequences of that sort of behaviour happening in public and how the police would be involved, particularly when the child is aged over ten years.

One child I worked with was terrified of the police but we did not know this until she had a violent outburst when our school policewoman came on one of her routine class visits. The child did not access the policewoman's lesson, which had been about 'stranger danger' but, once the child had calmed down, we found out that someone she knew had been to prison. We asked the child what she thought the police did in their role and her total understanding was that they just put people in prison.

We had several Behaviour Management sessions talking about what the police role in the community was, one of them being to visit local schools and talk to children about different dangers. We then arranged for the policewoman to return to the school just to talk to the child and to allow her to see her in a different way from the way they had previously perceived her. The policewoman was brilliant with the child and talked to her about the use of police dogs, helicopters, different police cars and all the various jobs police officers do. At the end of the meeting the policewoman presented the child with some lovely photos of the police helicopters, boats and cars as well as a special ruler for her pencil case, something the other children were later envious of. The next time the policewoman was due, we arranged for this child to meet her at reception and escort her to the classroom where the child sat and participated in the whole of her lesson. Problem solved.

Chapter 7

Small Group Work and Working One to One

Small groups

Some children with AS know very little about the condition and often have the belief that they are only person in the world with it, so when they realise that other children, and adults, have the same condition, it can be quite good for them. Emotional Literacy groups are a great place for this discussion to be initiated by staff. The children no longer feel so different or alone. They can relate to how other children may behave. Often, they don't know other children with AS, and AS groups can be beneficial for them, where they can talk about their feelings and how things upset them, etc. Pick your group of children carefully though. Sometimes, it may just have to be with a couple of children in the group as I have worked with various children with AS who are very different. Merely being in the room with a high-pitched or monotone child can upset the sensitive ears of the others.

However, it doesn't just have to be children with AS in your group. It could be that you have a small group for Anger Management, where you discuss how to help each other, get the children working in pairs, which children with AS can find difficult as they don't always like to take on others' views or opinions. Offer cheap rewards for achievements – stickers or, I have found, a drink of squash and a biscuit works really well at the end of a session.

Playing board games can also be a good way to get the children talking and seeing the child with AS in a different way. Getting children together who have previously had difficulties together can help them understand the child with AS better. They may even have things in common with them: pets, football, older or younger siblings, being born in the same month, etc.

Working one to one

Quite often, the opportunity arises in a school where you can work one to one, usually as a TA.[4] If you want to have more training, ask. Schools get a budget for staff training and it will benefit you and the children, so find out about enrolling on a course.

This is a hard job to do and at times it can feel that you really are out there on your own but at the same time it can be extremely rewarding although I wouldn't recommend working one to one all day every day with the same child. Not only do I not think it is a good idea for the staff member to be with the same child for a whole day, five days a week, but it is not always beneficial for the child. The member of staff can lose touch with what their

---

4   Some children in the UK are given one-to-one support and receive this from one TA throughout the day. Others may have two or more TAs throughout the day but still receive one-to-one support. One-to-one supporting can become quite intense and therefore TAs would normally be asked if they want to do this role.

TA role is all about (more than just one-to-one work). As far as the one-to-one child is concerned, he can become dependent on just one person, and possessive.

Ultimately, we are trying to teach these children the way the world works and we are trying to improve their understanding of it, so it is better for them to have other people working with them too. After all, what if their one-to-one person is ill, or decides to leave the school for whatever reason? The child needs to be able to feel comfortable with more than just one member of staff if he is to become more independent. However, the role can be shared so that one person does mornings and another afternoons and this is a great compromise all round. It has the advantage of allowing the child to get to know more than just one staff member quite well and in turn allows the staff members time to work with other children for the time they are not working one to one.

In the initial stages of working one to one, the support is there, but after a few weeks it *can* become as if you are the sole person responsible for the child and his behaviour. Quite often, when a staff member starts one-to-one work with a child, there is support from the class teacher, the head, the senior TA and perhaps other TAs. This support can be in the form of guidance, giving ideas or moral support and encouragement. However, sometimes this support can gradually be withdrawn as the people providing it continue with their own roles and make the assumption that the one-to-one TA is managing independently. It is during this time that you can be at your most vulnerable, when things don't go exactly to plan, and you start to feel you are to blame for problems that arise. You are left to deal with the minor difficulties whilst everyone else becomes more involved with the rest of the now settled class. However, this can also be very rewarding, because you have the time to build a working relationship with one child, you get to understand his needs more than anyone else on the staff list, and he gets to know you and learn to trust you (provided you follow through with things you say you will do). It also means that the rest of the staff trusts you to do your job independently.

If you are covering the child's breaks or lunchtimes, it will mean that you take your breaks at other times in the school day, meaning you will drink that cup of well-deserved coffee alone, without being able to catch up with your peers on what's going on in the rest of the school.

Personally, being the unsociable person that I can be, I rather enjoyed these quiet breaks and having time to reflect on what I was doing right, or wrong, and decide on my next course of action. If you are not like me, and enjoy others' company, make sure you have some time during each day to catch up with everyone you want to in the staff room, even if it's just to chat about what you watched on TV last night. It gives your mind something else to focus on for a while, other than just one child.

Although you will no doubt build a good working relationship with a child working one to one, it can become a problem if the boundaries are not made clear. The child may become cheeky if you allow your relationship to become too friendly. Remember, you are not there to be his friend; you are there to help him understand the world around him more easily. He has plenty of peers he can become friends with.

Over-familiarity can also make the child behave inappropriately toward you, perhaps giving you cuddles (some children with AS do like cuddles). This can be fine when the child is very young and needs some reassuring comfort, but can become quite inappropriate as the child gets older, and hormones start to kick in! Topics like this can be brought up in Behaviour Management sessions, perhaps using the 'stranger danger' heading, discussing who it is OK to cuddle, etc. The TA is not one of them.

Working one to one and getting this close to a child can leave you, and the child, with problems of misinterpretation.

Chapter 8

Breaktimes and Lunchtimes

Children with AS have difficulties with the Triad of Impairment (communication, socialisation and inflexibility of thought) and so they can have problems building and maintaining friendships, particularly with their peers. It may be that the child has problems at breaks because these are less structured times but also because she is not sure about how to keep and maintain friendships. In order to assist the child, perhaps an isolated area could be sought on the playground where this child plays with one or two selected friends as she learns how to play, compromise and share.

If it is difficult to find a patio or grass area, specifically for this child, then perhaps it is possible to mark out an area using cones. Other children will soon learn that this is a no go area unless they are playing with this specific child. Although children can be very cruel and blunt at times, they can also be very accommodating to children with behavioural difficulties.

If nobody wants to play with the child, perhaps offer an incentive, for example: 'Whoever plays with Gill today gets an extra five minutes break time.' This could be a starting point for introducing others to Gill's world and for Gill to understand more about the friendship process. Quite often though, you will find that a lot of the other children want to play with the child, especially if she has a designated area.

When the ultimate aim is for the child to be able to be integrated into the main playground for breaks and lunchtimes, there are a number of things we can do to assist the child with this. One of them is to teach her the ground rules for fair play. This includes taking turns and initially this can be practised in small group work in indoor activities such as board games, magnetic darts, dominoes, etc. If need be, set up a roster with the child's group of friends stating whose turn it is to choose what to play. If the child decides that she does not want to play when it is not her turn to choose the game, explain to her that it is then also fair for others not to want to play when it is her turn to choose. Sometimes breaks and lunchtimes will need to be well supervised for these children to enable you to explain why certain things may be happening and why certain children are doing or behaving a certain way. It is important to know that many children with ASDs do not understand how to read body language, facial expressions and tones of voice.

I have had to stop games before to explain to children with ASD that another child is getting upset due to their rough play, and that I can tell this because of the way that child is using her voice, or the look on her face or her whole body language. Once these things are pointed out to the child she is better able to understand what is happening.

It is also important to remember that sometimes, the child may want to spend some breaks on her own, simply because she wants to do her own thing, and this should be respected.

Chapter 9

Restraints

This is a controversial topic, but I believe that if restraints prevent a child harming himself or others, then it is a good thing to have them in place, provided, of course, staff are properly trained beforehand.

Some children's behaviour can be so challenging that to prevent injury to himself or others, it may be necessary to restrain the child for a short period of time. I have never yet met any member of staff who likes having to use this method of behavioural control but at times it seems the only way if everyone is to be kept safe. Strategies for Crisis Intervention and Prevention (SCIP) is a safe form of restraint to be used with children who are no longer in control of their behaviour. Training can be through the local council or through in-house training if there are people trained to deliver it. Although it is not an ideal course of action to have to physically restrain a child in this way, it can be essential if he is in danger of hurting himself or others due to his inability to control his behaviour.

A problem with using restraint in mainstream schools is that for mainstream children to witness a child being restrained can be quite frightening. The likelihood is that they will then go home and tell their parents what they have seen which could cause some concern amongst parents and this in turn could then snowball into something quite serious for the school's reputation. On the other hand, of course, there is the point that the school is being seen to include children with special needs and is using safely recognised measures to ensure that *all* children are kept safe.

However, if a child needs to be regularly restrained in a mainstream school, then perhaps mainstream is not the right place for him in the first place, and this is where it can be argued that the inclusion policy in the UK is failing.

I have had problems with using restraints when doing it with another adult who is not confident or totally happy about using it. This can lead to people getting hurt because the restraint is not doing what it was designed to do. I have been bitten numerous times because other restrainers have not held the child securely and safely. Some staff I have worked with have felt obliged to undergo the training, even though they have not felt comfortable about having to use it if the need arises. This should *never* be the case in mainstream schools. If a member of staff feels unhappy about using restraint they should be allowed to say 'No!' and not have it held against them. The staff should have the right to refuse.

When using SCIP, I have found that I am able to use it quite proficiently, (I've done it for over 12 years now) but even now, after the incident is over, the adrenalin rush goes and there can be a feeling of exhaustion and almost always that feeling of 'Could I have done something differently?', 'Should I have used the restraint when I did or should I have used it earlier/later?', 'Why didn't I recognise the antecedents?' or 'What were the antecedents in that incident?' In every case, I try to learn something positive about the incident, how I restrained, what the antecedents were, what I would do differently next time. Could the incident have been prevented? Nobody has all the answers to these questions, just know that you did what you believed to be the safest course of action at the time and move on from that.

Chapter 10

Role-Play and Puppets

Role-play

At first role-play can be quite intimidating, but lots of children enjoy it, especially if they get to be the one telling *you* what to do. It can be used to help explore problem-solving: it takes the emphasis of the problem away from the child *and* you don't have to be a drama student to try it! Role-play with children can be great fun, especially in small groups or one to one and this can be done in Behaviour Management sessions or Emotional Literacy sessions if your school does them. It gives the child time to practise strategies, and gives you time to allow her to be the adult while you practise the strategy also. It can be a very embarrassing thing to do, especially if you don't like amateur dramatics but try it out and enjoy the fun. The child will learn a lot from role-playing these situations as she is more able to tell you what *you* should do, when you play the child's part in the role-play and she plays the adult.

Also, it can give them a visual way of seeing how *not* to behave. For example, if the child has a problem taking turns, pretend to play a game, using a dice, and say it is her turn. Tell her it is role-play and you are not going to really play the game, but that *you* are going to do something wrong to see if she can see what it is you do wrong. As she is about to go, take the dice away and say that you want a go and proceed to roll the dice and move your counter. Then ask her how she felt about not being able to have her turn when it should have been her turn and how others might feel if they had to keep missing their turn because someone else kept pushing in and taking a go when it was not their turn. By taking the initial emphasis away from her she will be much better able to see what problems not taking turns can cause.

Role-play can be used for practising many situations in one-to-one work or small group work. For example, situations to practise could include asking other children if they (the child with AS) can join in, visiting another teacher on an errand, or lining up without pushing in – especially if she gets to be the person doing it right.

It is often a good idea for you to role-play a situation and ask the child what you are doing wrong. Suppose the problem is that the child is constantly calling out and interrupting in class. You take on the role of the child and allow her to take on the role of the teacher, perhaps telling a story to the class. As she starts telling the story, you keep calling out. The child then tells you what you should be doing. In doing the role-play like this, you often find that the child knows what to do in such situations (she may tell you to wait and put your hand up) but may need help in achieving it, giving you both the opportunity to explore strategies further. It could also be another one for the Strategy Book (see Chapter 18).

Another use of role-play is to act out a situation with the child being the one that has had an injustice done to her, and then ask her how she felt about it. For instance: you and the child are lining up to go into the dinner hall, and the child is first in the line. You decide you want to be first in the line and push in front of the child, perhaps telling her 'I want to go first today!' Then, sit down with the child and ask her how it felt to have you pushing in, when she had been waiting patiently at the front. After she has told you, ask her how she thinks other people would feel if *she* pushed in.

Role-play can be a great way to help prepare the child for a visit outside school, or another situation, which may be coming up, for example: a visit to the library, a museum trip or a theatre group visiting your school to put on a pantomime.

Puppets

As with role-play, using puppets can be quite a scary thing for us to try when we first start, as we are never quite sure how the child/children will react – will she think we've completely lost the plot, not believe in the character, or will she play along with it? I prefer to use a puppet in a one-to-one situation where the puppet 'talks' only to me, or with a small group of children, again, with the puppet only 'talking' through me. If there are other puppets available, perhaps after the session, the children could have a go with them, but try to keep your puppet as yours, that way, the mystery of its character is still there.

Puppets are particularly good for using with younger children. They can be used solely by yourself, or as a reward to help the child complete an activity.

Shy puppets can work well with noisy younger children (I used a turtle puppet that stayed in his shell if the child was too noisy or misbehaving) and can encourage a child to quieten down. Sometimes, just putting a puppet on the child's desk may help her to settle and work as she believes the puppet is watching her. It sounds unbelievable that she can believe this, knowing that it is a puppet, but if it works, why not give it a go?

When I have used puppets before, I have told the child that the puppet only talks to me, so making it more intriguing for her. I have got the puppet to 'whisper' in my ear, making it more believable to the child, that the character only speaks to me. (It also means that you don't have to try your hand at being a ventriloquist!)

Puppets can also be used to discuss some of the problems a child or children may have – for example, if the child is having difficulty in the playground, the puppet could be used in a small group. You could get the puppet to whisper in your ear that she or he is very sad because they don't know how to join in games with others in the playground. Children in the group could give the puppet ideas of how to join in and the emphasis is then taken away from the child with this difficulty. Or maybe the child in question is too rough and the puppet could then take on the persona of a child who wants to play roughly. The children are usually very good, and kind, in giving advice in this way. Again, it takes the emphasis of the behaviour away from the child and enables her to feel less threatened about the issue being discussed.

Sometimes, the child may not want to talk directly to you, but will talk to the puppet, even though it is on your hand. She might want to talk to it about a problem or worry she has and you can then use a voice for the puppet to help the child solve the problem.

There are a huge number of puppets on the market but if money is limited, car boot sales and charity shops are a great place to start looking for some. Or maybe even your own attic. Schools often have summer and Christmas fetes so maybe you could have a stall to raise money for puppets, or maybe the Parent Teacher Association, or your school's equivalent, could allocate some money from monies raised at such events to go towards purchasing your puppets.

Chapter 11

Worksheets and Word Searches

There are many books on the market available to assist with Behaviour Management sessions. However, sometimes it can be possible to make up your own individual ones adapted for a specific child, for example, using the computer, create a table to make your own word searches using words that are relevant to your child. (There are also websites where you type in the words you want to use, the size of the word search and it makes it up for you! Try typing 'blank word search' into the search engine.) These can be used for Behaviour Management sessions or time-out, fun activities. For example, if your child has a special interest in Pokémon, put his favourite characters in a word search. It is literacy related! These can be a way for the child to calm down and refocus.

Worksheets don't have to be boring either, so try to make them fun and interesting to read and do. When printing them off the computer, you could put a small colour picture on to brighten them up. Put cloze statements in them. A cloze sentence is where part of the text is missing and the student is required to put in the missing word. For example:

The child wore a _____ on his head to keep his head warm.

On a worksheet of cloze statements, the missing words may be listed in a jumbled order at the top of the page. Or maybe you could put the answers in anagrams for the child to rearrange. For example:

1. You use this to help you calm down –
   YSGTTREA KOOB

The answer you want him to find is 'Strategy Book'. It just makes the learning more fun and helps him to concentrate for slightly longer periods of time, as well as reinforcing his learning.

2. You use these to help you stay out of
   trouble – **GRAEN LUSRE**

The answer is 'anger rules'. You can use the things you have been working on, and if he finds that too easy, try some anagrams for things you are going to be working on.

You can also make up question worksheets about a particular problem, using another name for the child. (I asked the child I was working with what name he would like me to use for the character.) So, if George, for example, has a problem queuing for the dinner hall, make a worksheet saying something like this:

> It was lunchtime and Addy really disliked having to wait for his dinner. He always used to push to the front of the queue and other children got really cross with him. Write some strategies for Addy to help him learn how to queue like the other children. Talk about how you think the other children could help Addy.

Chapter 12

Acronyms

Acronyms are a fun way of helping a child to realise her behaviours in a private sort of code. I have worked with several students with AS who have a problem with being bossy, which upsets other children and makes her less approachable by peers. Bossiness is a word everyone seems to understand. I had noticed that a particular child did not like being called bossy and it often made her more upset if someone called her that. So, during a Behaviour Management session, I mentioned to this pupil that I felt she not only had AS (which, incidentally, she already knew) but that I thought she had MOSS. She looked at me, puzzled, and then asked 'What's that?' I explained that it was Member Of Staff Syndrome, where a student thinks she is a staff member and therefore feels she has to tell others what to do. She laughed at this and from then on, instead of being called bossy, staff would say 'Are you having MOSS today?' to which she would smile and reply that she wasn't, and ultimately she stopped the bossy behaviour. She would also point out to us when she thought other children were having a 'MOSS' day!

Another acronym I have used is PTB days. These are when the child is having a day where she is Pushing The Boundaries, often when a supply teacher is in or the child is working with new staff or pupils, or with a member of staff she knows will not be firm with her. It was a code that the child and staff understood and the other children were eager to understand but were only told if the child with the problem agreed to divulge to peers what the code meant. Not telling the other children maybe made her feel special, that she knew something the other children didn't. I would not have a problem with her keeping our code a secret – these children are often made to feel like outcasts and if it makes them feel special then it's surely worth trying, but I would let other staff know what the code was.

Sometimes, it can be difficult to tell the difference between the AS behaviour and the average naughty child behaviour and there *is* a difference. During times when I have felt that the child was opting out because she didn't want to do the task as opposed to not being able to, I have called these Double O days or OO days – Opting Out days. Again, the child has understood that there is a difference and one particular child has even told *me* when it's a Double O day!

Perhaps you and the child you are working with can come up with your own acronyms.

Part III

DEALING WITH FEELINGS

Chapter 13

Anxieties

The anxieties of a child with AS can be more severe than the average child, due to the way he perceives the world around him. It is therefore our job to help lessen those concerns for him and we can do that in a number of ways.

Initially, we need to start to build a positive relationship with him. This can be by doing fun activities, perhaps during breaktimes, such as a board game or reading a book or favourite comic together, and this time can be built into the timetable so that you both get the chance to get to know each other better. Allow the child to choose the activity but also make sure that he goes along with your ideas for an activity too. This will help him when turn-taking with peers.

It may be that the child has anxieties about certain areas in school, perhaps the school hall or the library. This can be eased by taking photos around the school of all the areas, ones that cause anxieties and ones that do not, and making a kind of scrap book or photo album with the pictures. Together you could type a few sentences about each photo, and take occasional trips to the rooms when they are quiet to get the child used to the room. Perhaps he could show the album to his class or to a new child at the school. This would help build his confidence and self-esteem. Visit the different classes or rooms with the child at various times of the day, perhaps for trivial things like collecting a book, or delivering a written message (possibly prearranged by you) to someone in the room, just so he gets used to going into that room and can see that nothing bad is going to happen.

It may be that the child is anxious about certain members of staff. In this case, arrange a time when the child can have an informal chat with the staff member and talk about fun things, like their pets or hobbies. This allows the child to see the member of staff as something other than this person he is afraid of. It may be the person has a moustache (worrying if it is a female teacher!) or is very tall or has a loud or deep voice or that he or she just reminds him of someone else. It could be any number of things and by having an informal chat with the staff member it can help to lessen the child's concerns.

Chapter 14

Managing Anger with Exercise

As I have said, many children with ASDs may also have another diagnosis attached, such as ADHD. I have found that, on occasions, these children can benefit from getting extra exercise to help them calm down and focus more easily. Exercise can also help reduce physical incidents. If you imagine a child who can regularly go from being very calm (let's call that a '0') to very angry (let's call that a '10') within seconds, then by the time she has reached the '10' stage she has completely lost control and is incapable of listening to anything you say. It is therefore futile to try to reason or redirect her at this stage and you will have to wait until she has calmed down to discuss anything with her. However, if you build some form of physical exercise into her daily programme (preferably in the mornings) when she does get cross, it takes her longer to reach a level 10, therefore giving you a bit more time to redirect her or reason with her before she totally loses her self-control.

If the child is becoming over-excited before a lesson or seems to have a surplus amount of energy, why not take her outside onto the playing field and let her run around the track for five minutes to burn some of it off? It may be that there is a set time of day when she has extra energy and is unable to sit quietly to do work without disrupting the other children. In this case you could make exercise part of her daily routine. So, for example, if the child is unsettled before maths each morning, build it into her timetable that she has a ten-minute run before each maths lesson. If she does not like running, how about skipping, or a musical aerobic-type exercise or using a hoop around the waist and keeping it up or kicking a football back and forth to you?

It may be that there are several children who could benefit from this type of energy release and it could be used for a group of students for five or ten minutes each time.

There are also many smaller exercises that children can do to help them remain on task and again, these can be used for more than one child. They are called Brain Gym® activities (see www.braingym.org.uk for information) and many schools now use them for whole classes, particularly for the younger children. They involve stopping the class, if they have become a bit fidgety for example, and doing tasks like standing up behind a chair in silence, writing their name in the air with the right index finger, then the left index finger, an elbow, a knee and finally with their bottom. It's a fun way to help the children refocus. After several different exercises like these (and there are books out there on a wide range of Brain Gym activities) the children then return to their work and are better able to concentrate.

There is also training on Brain Gym exercises and maybe this is something that your school could look into (details can be found by putting Brain Gym in the computer search engine). They are great fun to try yourself and see what your co-ordination is like!

If exercise is not an option but the child is becoming increasingly unsettled, try redirecting her attention elsewhere. You could use one of her Space Cards (see Chapter 19) to call her out of class and get her to run an errand such as taking the register back to the main office, or holding some work while you put it up on a display board, or even helping to tidy the PE cupboard. These are all just ideas that I have used and that have worked, but adapt them to suit your child, yourself and your school. Get your imagination working. It's fun.

Chapter 15

Emotions – The Feelings Book

The Feelings Book is a cheap exercise book and can have a smiley face and a sad face coloured on the front of it. Inside, you put the date and leave the book where the child knows they can find it. It is a private book for you and him to use to communicate. Like most of us, sometimes the child with AS does not feel able to verbalise his feelings. Therefore, the idea of this book is to allow him to draw a picture of a sad or smiley face in the book each morning or afternoon to show how he feels. If he draws a sad face it means that he is not happy that day for whatever reason and therefore it would be a good idea to take him out for a chat. Some staff may not think this is a good idea, as the child will miss part of the lesson. But surely it is better to sort the child's worries and concerns as early as possible before they escalate.

If the child is unable to tell you verbally what is wrong, encourage him to draw, or write, what is troubling him. You can give him confidence by allowing him to know that it is safe for him to tell you what is wrong, and by not telling him off when he does. For example, if the child tells you he is upset because he hit his sister that morning, and then Mummy told him off and took his computer game away, don't tell him that you would have done the same if your child had behaved like that, even it is true. Tell him that there are other ways of dealing with issues, and reinforce the Behaviour Management strategies and Anger Rules (see p.46). Give him other alternatives to think about if the sister upsets him again. What he needs from you is support and guidance, not for you to be their parent or carer. They have them already.

It may also be said that maybe all children need time for this, but my point is that the behaviours of the child with AS can become quite extreme if he feels that he is not being understood, or cannot work out a way to deal with his anxieties alone, whereas the average child is able to wait and put his feelings on hold a while, perhaps until breaktime.

Sometimes, just the fact that the child is unhappy can be the antecedent, which, if not addressed soon enough, can escalate into a full incident. Why put yourself and the child through a bad day just because you didn't spend a few minutes finding out how he was feeling that morning?

Part IV

IDEAS FOR VISUAL LEARNERS

Chapter 16

Visual Learners

Many children with an ASD have poor auditory process-
ing skills and benefit from visual cues. Some children
prefer to see their daily timetable in pictorial form, as
shown in Figure 16.1, as it aids their comprehension of
the activities for the day.

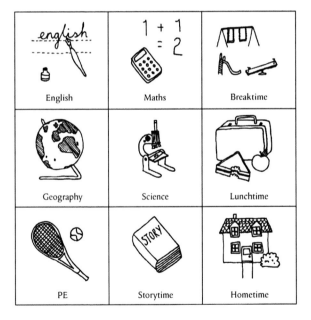

Figure 16.1 Example of a timetable in pictorial form

The timetable can be made up using pictures from clipart on the computer, using photographs taken at the school, or by using a specific computer programme for visual timetables, such as Communicate In Print (www.widgit. com/inprint). The pictures and timetable will last longer if laminated. Each picture should be cut out as a separate piece and Velcro stuck on the back. In each square of the timetable should be stuck the opposite pieces of Velcro to attach the lesson pictures when in use. If it is used by the whole class, the timetable could be a monitor's job to change on a daily basis.

Other visual cues can include clearly and concisely written class rules, rules for games, or reminders of what to put in their school bag each morning which can help develop their independent organisational skills.

Chapter 17

Oops! Cards

Many children with AS find change extremely difficult to cope with. This is where the Oops! Card can come into play. I had never heard of these before going on a course about AS when I was told about a school that had used them with their children. I immediately went back and we tried them out and they proved to be very effective. Again, they can be made up on the computer to your own design and are used by the adult but the child could be involved, if you so choose. They are useful for all children in the classroom, not just the child with AS. If you decide on using the Oops! Card, maybe you could take the child out of class for a short time and he could help design the card. He might then be keener to see it used effectively.

For example, see Figure 17.1.

Figure 17.1 Example of an Oops! Card

These cards can be used if there is a change to the timetable, or if there is a change to staffing or if an unexpected visitor is arriving which had not been scheduled. This allows the child time to understand that something is not going to be the same that day. An Oops! Card is used on a visual timetable by putting it in the place of the activity that will not be happening. This can be placed on the timetable by the teacher, or by the child with AS at the request of the teacher or TA. If there is more than one change to the day's activities it may be necessary to use more than one Oops! Card on the timetable at the same time. If the teacher or TA chooses, they can involve the child in displaying the cards on the white board, giving him a monitoring role and giving his self-esteem a boost. If there is a change to the afternoon timetable then display the Oops! Card as early as possible so the child can use his strategies to enable him to deal with the situation more effectively. It may be easier for the child to be taken aside and told of the changes verbally before asking him to display the Oops! Card and the teacher telling the rest of the class of the change. This is a strategy that can help everyone in the class, including the staff! Remember though, that all these strategies will take time to get used to so don't get upset if they don't work every time. Sometimes, we ourselves have to adapt our own strategies in life and this is no different for the child with AS.

Chapter 18

The Strategy Book

Children with an ASD may have difficulty, as we may all have at times, understanding different ways to do things which may be more appropriate and acceptable. Therefore, the Strategy Book can be a cheap and effective way to show them.

The book shows the child that she has other choices than using an unacceptable behaviour. A child with AS (and some without) is not always able to understand initially that there are other ways to solve a problem, other than to lash out, and is often keen to be taught other ways and be shown other ideas. Eventually, the plan should be that the child herself can come up with her own ideas and strategies, initially writing them in her book, then, over time, adapting them and being confident and competent enough to think one through and use it without the need to see it visually on paper.

So, bearing all that in mind and using a cheap exercise book (every school should have one somewhere), draw a shape in the middle of the page. If, for example, the problem is that the child has hit someone when she was cross with him or her, write in the middle of the shape an alternative statement, such as: 'Instead of hitting someone when I am angry, I could...' Then draw lines, usually about three or four, out from the shape in different directions. For each line, help the child to think of a different way she could have managed the situation better. Initially, she may not know any other way than to lash out, in which case it will be down to you to give the child some strategies.

This will then form a visual strategy the child can refer to each time the situation arises. The child must be allowed full access to the book at all times, either at her table or in her quiet area. Each time a new problem arises, add another strategy page to the book. For examples, see Figure 18.1.

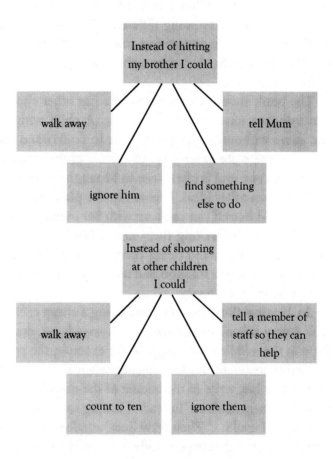

Figure 18.1 Examples of pages in a Strategy Book

The child can even decorate the cover and colour in each shape as it gets filled, so it feels more personal to her. Colouring with coloured pencils (felt pens often go straight through to the next page) can also be a relaxing and calming activity. It may be that several problems arise at once. This is not a problem, it just means drawing more shapes for each problem in the book.

The main picture does not have to be a shape. I am not particularly artistic, favouring matchstick men to bodied characters, and so I chose a shape but if the child you are working with likes dinosaurs and you, or she, are artistic and happy to take the time to draw the outline of a dinosaur, then try that. Or maybe they like bouncy castles, then you could draw a bouncy castle with the towers at the top, which could point to the strategies. The possibilities are endless. If the child likes sport, you could draw different types of sports balls, or if she likes nature, draw some flowers with the strategies in the petals. Be creative and work with the child – it's great fun and can help keep you young!

I have worked with children who have had over 40 strategies in their book, for things like:

Instead of spitting, I could...

Instead of picking my nose in public, I could...

If I do not understand my work in class, I could...

If two people give me different instructions at the same time, I could...

Instead of swearing, I could...

If there is a supply teacher in class, I could...

If my brother upsets me before I come into school, I could...

If I am sad, I could...

If I am worried about something, I could...

When there is a change in my timetable, I could...

...and many others.

Then, as she becomes more adept at using different strategies, she will get to a stage where they are all covered by one strategy:

Use my strategies without prompts.

One of the strategies I worked on with one child was: 'Instead of swearing, I could ... say the word in my head.' I asked the girl if she could try that using some role-play, bearing in mind she had recently used the 'f' word in the playground. She said that she didn't think she would be able to do that. I told her to give it a try, and to imagine I had upset her and to swear at me in her head, but not let the words come out of her mouth. As I looked at her, her face and mouth went very rigid, her cheeks puce, her eyebrows furrowed and her eyes bore into mine, but she said nothing. I then asked her if she had just sworn at me and she smiled and said 'Yep'. I then congratulated her for using a new strategy and told her that although she had sworn at me it had not come out of her mouth and therefore, since she hadn't actually said it, I couldn't tell her off for it. A strategy some adults could do with learning!

Knowing and testing a child's abilities to problem solve can be a case of trial and error. We can help empower children by enabling them to understand ways to react to anger that are more appropriate and they are likely to be more willing to try as they trust us to be right. This is where the real test of the Strategy Book comes in.

After working with a child for over a year, she was extremely rude to me and then demanded I help her. I told her that I had no intention of helping her until she had put right the fact she had upset me. She shouted at me that she didn't know how. I then silently handed her her Strategy Book as she sat under a tree in the school grounds. I walked away, but watched her from a distance. After reading through all her strategies, she shouted 'That was no help, there's not one in there for that!' I briefly told her to adapt one of them. After several minutes flicking through her book, she called out, very calmly 'OK, I need some card and some crayons though.' I gave her what she required and sat back and waited. Some time later, she came out from under the tree and handed me a hand-made card, which said 'Sorry for being rood' (rude). This was the first time she had adapted one of the strategies for a slightly different problem and we discussed how well she had done in achieving that and reinforced that strategies could be adapted if necessary.

Chapter 19

Cards and Rewards

▬ ▬ ▬ ▬ ▬ ▬ ▬ ▬ ▬ ▬ ▬

Cards are another cheap but effective resource.

Firstly, the Space Card: so called as it refers to the child being given space and often has the picture symbol of something relating to space, such as an astronaut or planet, or a field or an ocean. This card is adult initiated. The cards can be laminated and should be about the size of a credit card so they are able to fit in pockets. If the child does not like astronauts, then a picture of a field with a rabbit or pony in could be used instead. These can be made up on the computer, put onto card and laminated. Figure 19.1 shows examples of pictures you could use.

Figure 19.1 Examples of Space Cards

Each member of staff working with the child should have their own Space Cards that the child can recognise. They may all have the same picture on them or there may be a different picture on each card, but ensure the child knows what the different pictures are when you make them so he knows that when they are used it is for him to take time-out. For example, if planets are used, there may be one card with a picture of Venus on and another of Jupiter on.

These cards can be used to redirect a child and can also be a way of earning a reward. If the child is becoming cross, the teacher or TA can hold a Space Card up and alert the child to the fact it is being shown. It may be a case of calling the child's name, though not at the top of your voice in front of the whole class, or just placing it on the table in front of him. The idea is that the child calmly goes to the person holding the card and is spoken to in order to find a solution to what is troubling him. It may be that the member of staff asks him to go to his bay for some time-out. If the child responds appropriately to the card and goes to the member of staff then he earns his reward, whatever that may be. Remember, rewards do not have to be expensive. It may be that the child likes computers. Therefore, it may be that you make up a card with 20 pictures of a computer on, and each computer has to have an earned sticker (or stamp) on. When the child has earned 20 stickers or stamps for responding to the Space Card being used, he can go, for example, on the computer for 20 minutes and play a game of his choice. It may be that he loves playing football, in which case the card could have 20 balls on and once each ball has an earned sticker or stamp on, the child has earned 20 minutes playing football with a friend during lesson time. What better incentive for him to achieve than that! Some cereal packets still give free gifts in them and these could be used as rewards. Get the rest of the staff to collect them too.

To get the child to respond to the cards to start with, it is important that they are seen as a positive thing. For example, use one to get the child to receive praise for a piece of work, or perhaps just to return the register, or ask him a question about his choice of reading book. Always ensure he receives his sticker to put on his card to enable him to achieve his reward, whether it is for responding to a positive thing or responding to the card when he is upset. And always remember to make sure he gets his reward when he has earned it so he can see the result of his good behaviour and, again, trusts that you will do what you say.

Then there is the Referee Card or Time Out Card. This is a card of similar size but is child initiated. It doesn't have to be called a Referee Card and the child could decide what he wants to call it. Again, the design of the card could be changed to suit the child, for example, use pink card for a girl if they feel the card is not girly enough.

Again, these can be made up on the computer, using a picture symbol, or using pictures from a comic or magazine. One child I worked with wanted pictures of Rugby World Cup hero Jonny Wilkinson (I was quite happy with his choice too!) and we managed to get some from the internet, stuck them each onto a piece of card and laminated them. Make sure you have enough spare copies in case they get lost, or left at home. For examples, see Figure 19.2.

These cards are child initiated, for when he requires help, wants some time-out or needs to talk to the teacher or TA. There may or may not be a reward for these but if there are too many rewards available they become less effective.

Figure 19.2 Examples of Time-Out Card and Referee Card

The child may need reminding to always have a card in his pocket or available at his table. Therefore, it is useful to have a good supply handy in case he forgets or loses them and get into the habit of checking with the child each morning that he has a card in his pocket or pencil case.

We had several different pictures of Jonny but the child knew that each card was for the same thing – getting our attention in an appropriate way.

For these cards to be used effectively, you might consider seating the child as near to the door as possible so he has a quick and easy exit route to go for his time-out and the adult can then follow. If the child has to manoeuvre past a member of staff or their peers, in order to gain exit, he could become more anxious due to being more noticed and this in turn could disrupt the rest of the class. This is a simple, but effective, strategy to put in place right from the start.

Chapter 20

Sand and Egg Timers

Sand timers or egg timers can often be found in amongst the maths resources and can be used effectively for timing an activity the child finds difficult. If you do not have any in school, egg timers in all sorts of shapes can be found quite cheaply at car boot fairs or yard sales.

They are visual and the child can understand that time is moving. They can be bought for various times, for example, 30 seconds, one minute, five minutes and ten minutes. If, for example, a child *never* attends music, tell her that she is required to do so for five minutes in the next music lesson. After she has done that, she can leave and go to her bay. She could do another activity, or this may be a good time to do a Behaviour Management session (see Chapter 6).

Sand or egg timers can also be used for when the child needs some time-out from a game, for example. So, if the child is becoming unsettled in a playground game with their peers, suggest she goes to an area, not necessarily her bay, and uses a sand or egg timer. When the sand has run through, or the timer pings, and provided the child has calmed down, she can then return to the game. This could be used for all the children in the game as it may not be just the child with AS who is getting over-excited, as many school-children are unable to cope with losing in a game and may become cross and unsettled. If the timers are used for activities like this it can show the child that she is being treated the same as her peers.

A well-used statement I have heard, and used myself successfully, is: 'When you have done this, then you can do that.' The use of the sand timers is great for such times.

Often, a child cannot see the point of doing a particular piece of work, for example she may not see the point in doing maths. The trick is to try to find a practical reason for doing the activity, such as learning how to tell the time. If she can't tell the time she will be late getting to work when she is older, then she won't be able to earn enough money for those nice things she likes to eat. Or, if reading is a problem, find a topic she is interested in. Many children do not like this activity, but without being able to read how will she know if she is buying the correct things in the supermarket, or whether her favourite TV programme is on that week, or if she has been invited to a party or won a competition or know what her latest certificate is for?

A child I worked with absolutely loathed reading and avoided it as much as she could. So I brought in the sports pages of a national newspaper, which had been covering the Rugby World Cup (which she and I were doing a project on during lunchtimes), and she read some of the reports without actually realising she was reading! Another good way to get children reading is to show them the Guinness World Records book, which is full of small fascinating facts. Just flick through and get the child to read a piece about something that interests her. Again, use the five-minute sand or egg timer to start with.

Chapter 21

The Home/ School Diary

This is a very important, yet cheap, resource that can be made in school and adapted for each child. It allows communication between the parents and school about the child. It is a book that goes home every evening and is returned to school each morning. The staff dealing with the child throughout the day enter relevant comments in it. It may be that the child does not like what has been written in it, particularly if it has comments about his negative behaviour in it. So it may be that instead of it being put into his school bag, on some days it might be best to hand it to whoever is collecting the child from school.

Many children, not just children with AS, are often unable to understand that parents and school staff communicate about them. Therefore, there can be a tendency for the child to play one off against the other. With the use of the Home/School Diary this can be minimised. It builds a relationship, and understanding, between the parents and staff dealing with the child. It means that both sides can inform the other of difficulties and achievements on a daily basis, with both being able to support the other and sometimes advise on how they have dealt with particular problems. At this point, I would like to point out that the children who I have seen progress the most are those whose parents work with the school and where the school works with the parents. If they disagree, they must do it out of earshot of the child as this will only add to his anxieties. Figure 21.1 is an example of a primary school child's Home/School Diary.

The parent comment can go at the start or end of the page. Both school and parents need to acknowledge what the other is saying.

If you are working with an older child, then you could make the diary look more like a Filofax by adding different sections. For example, a section for school notes, another for the parents' notes and a further section for the child's notes. Again, it is simple enough to make, it just takes a little thought and time. TAs should be allowed time to prepare resources during their normal working day.

This is an excellent way to communicate, along with regular parental meetings, which can also be beneficial, particularly if the parents are not very literate or the teaching staff are not very clear in their handwriting. This could be done on a particular day each week when the teacher/TA can explain how the child is doing to the parent and each could exchange ideas and thoughts. The child may be invited in for some of the meeting to give his views.

The idea of these meetings and the diary is that the child understands that *everyone* is working at trying to help him to achieve his full potential.

ACTIVITY	Staff comments	SIGNED BY
Register	Settled well and came up with good ideas for Brain Gym activity	Mr A
Assembly	Fidgeted but managed to stay in for half the time. Good progress.	Miss B
Lessons 1 and 2	Started well. Problem over handwriting but used Referee Card and took herself out to her bay. Returned and completed work.	Mr A
Breaktime	Played alone as did not want to play what others were playing. This is an area we need to work on so she can make friends.	Miss B
Lessons 3 and 4	Worked really hard in maths and earned a credit for completing her work and for it being so neat.	Mr C
Lunchtime	Was brought in for being too rough. We talked about how we could change this behaviour so that she would enjoy breaks more.	Miss B
Lesson 5	During Behaviour Management, we talked about how she could make more friends. New strategy in book.	Miss B
Breaktime	Wanted to walk round and chat with me so we chatted about our weekends.	Miss B

Lesson 6	Seemed to enjoy DT but got cross when unable to use equipment as others were there first. Space Card used and she calmed quickly.	Mr A
Parent Comments	Have suggested G having a friend home for tea as we thought this might help with the friendship/turn-taking problems. Any ideas who might be a good choice?	Mum

Figure 21.1 Example of a Home/School Diary

Chapter 22

The Good Book

Children with AS often have very low self-esteem and put a lot of pressure on themselves to get things right every time and without making any mistakes. Quite often they have been bullied by peers, or adults, due to their lack of understanding of the social world around them, where others have failed to appreciate just how difficult this actually is for them. They may also have been told they are stupid, or bad, whereas it would have been better for others to have labelled their behaviour, not them. They develop low self-esteem and are reluctant to understand that they do actually do a lot of things right.

This is where the Good Book comes in. Again, another exercise book, and by now you may be thinking, 'Crikey, where are we going to keep all these books and surely it will be confusing for the child to have them all?' If you introduce them all at once then it probably will be. However, each book is a *very* important one and each serves its own purpose.

Allow the child to decorate the book with pictures of their choice: fast cars, footballers, flowers, dinosaurs, etc. – as it is *their* Good Book. If you have some sticky-backed plastic to cover it in, so much the better, as it will help to preserve this valuable self-esteem boosting book.

Every day, put the date in the book. At the end of every day, under the date, write something good that the child has done that day. Even if the child has had a foul day, there is always something she has done well. It could be that she hung her coat on her peg when she came into school that morning. The fact that she then caused mayhem in school the rest of the time and had to be sent home is irrelevant. The fact is, she *had* done something well and it needs to be recorded. Often, a child with AS feels very negative about herself and her poor behaviour, and she is unable to see the good in herself. This book helps her to see that, actually, she is doing a lot of things right.

Never, ever, put negative comments in this book. It is a book to boost her self-esteem and morale and is something that the child can look at when she is taking time out, feeling sad or just wants to feel good.

It may seem that this, and the other resources and ideas are time consuming, but if your school policy has anything in it about 'helping everyone to achieve their full potential' then surely they are worth trying and giving a little bit of time to.

Over time, this book becomes a catalogue of events that are *all* about the child doing things the right way. So, no matter how bad a day the child seems to have had, there will always be at least one thing she has done right. For another example, she may come into school and push past others in the cloakroom, then shout at people and swear at someone, *but* she may have only used one swear word today, whereas yesterday she used three. It doesn't take long to build up the contents in this book but if, one day, you are stuck for something to write in it, ask your peers if they have seen the child doing something positive today – the dinner lady, teachers, secretary, and maintenance man. Table 22.1 is an example of what the inside of a Good Book could look like:

Table 22.1 Example of a section from a Good Book

12th July	Gill only called out once in class today which is a great improvement.
13th July	Gill waited in the lunch queue today with the rest of her class.
14th July	Gill stayed in for ten minutes of assembly this morning, which is five minutes more than she has ever managed before. Huge progress.
15th July	Gill played nicely with two children during morning break and they both want to play catch with her at break again tomorrow.
16th July	When another child accidentally pushed into Gill at breaktime and apologised, Gill smiled and said it was OK.
17th July	Gill played a board game with another child today and took turns equally. She also let the other child throw the dice first.

As with the Strategy Book, the child could decorate it with pictures cut out of magazines or drawings if she wants to personalise it, again during Behaviour Management sessions. It is a nice tool for a child to look at when she is feeling down about herself or her recent behaviour, and serves as a visual reminder to show her that she does manage to do good things every day. Not only is it positive for the child and staff to see this book get longer and longer as more things are added, but it is a good tool to show parents as well. Quite often they have had a lot of negative feedback about their child so to have someone make a point of finding something positive about their child can be a huge boost for them, showing them that their child is making some progress.

Chapter 23

Visual Conversations

Another powerful tool for visual learning is visual conversations. These are a way to show a child or young adult that something is not right and to let him see it without the initial emphasis being on him.

I learned how to use visual conversations at a special school I worked at. They are an excellent way of enabling the child to see a situation through an observer's eyes and therefore gain a better understanding of how others view his behaviours. The aim is to get the child to recognise the behaviour without any blame being put in his direction – once he can understand how others behave and how his behaviour is viewed by others, then he is better able to understand the impact his own behaviour has on the people around him. Here is an example of one visual conversation held.

The child I was working with had been having problems with outbursts and other children had been upset about them. I had a small white board and pen and drew a picture (Figure 23.1) on the board whilst he was looking around the room at others. He was an inquisitive child and, though I had said nothing, he was interested to know what I was doing. He watched as I drew (not my forte!) and asked what it was.

Figure 23.1 Visual conversation: Picture 1

I told him that the little girl in the picture had had an argument at home before breakfast and had come into school really upset and angry that morning, but she didn't tell anyone. I told him that she went into class, and found the children were doing Design and Technology. Immediately, the boy folded his arms across his chest and said quite firmly, 'Well, I don't think that was a safe thing to do with tools around.' I told him she was still really cross and left the room and went and found a class that were doing PE. The little girl took their ball away. I asked the boy what he thought the other children in the PE group would have been feeling. He huffed a bit and shook his head and said, 'Well, they'd be upset because they wouldn't be able to play their game because they no longer have a ball and they only get PE twice a week.' At this stage I sensed that he was getting cross at this girl's behaviour. I then told him that after she had thrown the ball away, the girl had gone into an art class and torn up a picture another little girl had painted for her mummy. I told him that the girl with the painting, and her friend, had watched the other girl tear her painting up. I asked what he thought the little girl and her friend would think. He replied, 'Well, the girl would be really upset because she had spent a lot of time doing a picture for her mum and her friend wouldn't like seeing her friend upset so she would be upset too.' He continued looking at the picture but moved back a couple of feet. After a few seconds, he asked, 'Is that what I'm like?'

From then on, we were able to talk about how his actions impacted on others and he was able to understand this because the visual conversation took the 'blame' away from him. He was able to see how someone else's behaviour affected others and was then able to understand his behaviour better.

Most schools do visits outside in the local community and this can be a time when inappropriate behaviours can be exhibited. Visual conversations can also be used to show a child how the public view certain behaviours, again, using the same idea as above.

During a Behaviour Management session, draw a visual conversation making sure the child is not the person in it. For example, if you are working with a girl, make the pictures of boys, or vice versa. Use a problem that can happen, though not necessarily one that has happened with this child.

The visual conversation in Figure 23.2 shows a child pushing another child. Watching what is happening is an old man across the street.

Figure 23.2 Visual conversation: Picture 2

Your conversation could be something like this:

> Some school children are out in the local high street doing a survey with the rest of their class and teachers. Child A wants to do the writing for their group but Child B had been chosen by the rest of the group to do the writing. Child A was not happy with this and, when the teacher wasn't looking, pushed Child B to the ground. Child A did not notice the old man across the street watching them.

- What do you think the old man (and anyone else who was around) was thinking?

- How did Child A's behaviour reflect on the school?

- What do you think the man thought of Child A?

- What do you think the old man did? (Phone the school, phone the police, etc.)

- How do you think Child B would feel, after the rest of the group had voted for him to do the writing?

- How do you think Child A felt?

- How do you think the rest of the group felt about what had happened?

- What do you think would happen when they got back to school?

- What could Child A do differently?

- What do you think Child A achieved from pushing the other child?

If the child is unable to come up with relevant answers, help him by telling him what you think would be the answers. By talking about issues in this way, the child is able to get another perspective on happenings around him.

Part V

ASSESSING CHILDREN WITH ASPERGER SYNDROME

Chapter 24

Record Keeping

Once you start working with the child, keep notes, and clear records, of behaviours shown. Not only is it beneficial for yourself to look at what behaviours have occurred and how you or others have dealt with them, but it is also a good record for the parents. For your part, it may prove really useful should you decide to do any training relevant to working with children or attend any training courses where you could put your views across and have the paperwork to back up your work and ideas. As for the parents in the UK, it may be because the parents want to go for a Statutory Assessment of their child's needs in order to get them a Statement of Educational Needs that will enable the child to have the support they need in school. Statements are legal documents and what is stated in them should happen. Unfortunately, some school staff believe that because a child is academically able she does not need a statement. I do not necessarily agree. Children with an ASD have difficulties in social and communication skills and inflexibility of thought, and this can be detrimental to their whole well-being if not acknowledged and worked with. It can also affect an individual's adult life – if she has masses of academic qualifications but she cannot hold down a job or friendship due to a lack of social and communication skills and her rigid way of thinking, then the exam results will not necessarily benefit her. Therefore her qualifications were possibly more for the school's needs than the child's. Schools need to be seeing the child as a whole – not just a machine to acquire knowledge for tests and exams which look good in league tables. You are dealing with people, little people who are vulnerable and need your support in more than academic ways.

Another common problem, where the school refuses to accept the parent's wish for a Statutory Assessment, is when the child exhibits little or no negative behaviours in school but does so when she gets home. This can be because the child has struggled all day at school to be good and understand what is going on around her. Then by the time she gets home she is fit to burst with sheer frustration, and knows that at home, someone under-stands her needs and understands her enough to accept her even when she temporarily loses her self-control. Un-fortunately, parents and siblings often suffer emotionally, and physically, because of it. Schools should be talking to parents when parents express this concern. They should support what they are saying by trying to give the child an outlet at school to express her worries so that they can alleviate (1) the child's anxieties and (2) the stress this causes at home. It may be that the child is struggling with the work or finding it too easy, or she has problems finding suitable friends at breaks and lunchtimes, or that she is upset by the level of noise around her or in certain classes, or she could be confused about what is expected of her as a pupil or as a friend or classmate. Remember, these children have deficits in social and communication skills and just because they are quiet and well behaved at school, it does not mean they are happy or comfortable with their surroundings. Teaching these children is not just about teaching them academically, it is about gently explaining the world around them and how it works. It is about differentiation which, from the amount of calls I get at work from anxious parents, is not happening as often as it should be.

Recording of incident reports

It is a good idea to write reports of incidents that happen so that you can build a picture of the child's behaviours. For me, an incident would be where the child had an outburst involving any of the following behaviours:

- *Verbal abuse* (VA): this can be anything from telling staff to shut up, to swearing.

- *Physical attack* (PA): this can be pushing, hitting, kicking, throwing an object, spitting, etc.

- *Absconding* (A): when the child leaves school grounds or the areas where she is allowed.

- *Non-compliance* (NC): when a child deliberately refuses to comply with the instruction of the staff.

- *Disruptive behaviour* (DB): this is when the child's behaviour disrupts the learning or activities of others.

These are just some of the behaviours and your child may have others that she exhibits which you could put on your forms. Some people find it easier to type up their reports. They should always include certain information; this information can then be used to help determine key areas of concern.

A few important things to remember when dealing with incidents

- Don't take them personally: although the child is upset and you are dealing with it, it is probably her understanding of a situation that is making her upset, not you. Deal with the incident and move on positively.

- If the child is shouting at you to say or do something, tell her calmly, 'When you are calm, then I will talk to you.' If she continues, repeat your statement again, calmly, until she is calm. Remember though, it could take some time for her to calm down enough for her to stop shouting and listen. During her shouting episode, remain quiet and calm, only saying, 'When you are calm, then I will speak to you.' Once she has calmed down, talk to the child but if she starts to get cross again, repeat the phrase and walk away a few paces until she is ready to try again.

- It is best if only one person is doing the talking to the child. If two or more people start saying things to the child then she can become confused and more anxious. When she has calmed down enough to talk reasonably again, then another person can join the conversation. Ideally though, let the person dealing with the incident in the first place deal with it. If you disagree with what that person has said or done, then discuss it with him later, *not* in front of the child, or call him over for a quiet chat and discuss your concerns.

- Know your child: if the child likes spending time at home, make sure that the behaviour is not just a ploy to get her parents to pick her up for an exclusion/suspension. This could reinforce poor behaviours. If the child does not like being sent home, then the child is unlikely to use poor behaviour as a tool to be sent home and therefore there will be an underlying reason for the behaviour.

School staff can make up the incident report themselves and then a supply can be photocopied. They should include the following information:

- Day
- Date
- Time of incident
- Lesson
- Type of incident
- Pupils involved
- Staff involved
- Witnesses
- What happened?
- Why do you think it happened?
- What, in your opinion, could be done to prevent this happening again?

When you have this information, you have the data needed for the graphs to be used at reviews and assessments, but more of that later.

The members of staff who witnessed the incident should write their *unbiased* account of what happened. By unbiased, I mean that you write exactly what you saw and heard, not what you interpret it to be and not why you think it happened. That comes later. Therefore, you shouldn't be writing 'I saw Gill hit Fred because...' You don't know the reason Gill hit Fred, you are only speculating. Unless of course Gill said 'I'm hitting Fred because...' which is highly unlikely.

Try not to speculate about a child's AS either. For example 'It was due to Gill's AS that she hit Fred.' This is your opinion and, though the incident may be due to Gill's AS, it is not necessarily a fact. The AS itself does not make the child have an incident, but it is the way the child interprets things, because of her AS, that can make her unsettled. It is important to remember that the AS is a condition that can be understood, if we try, and not a condition that means the child is unwilling to play by the rules.

You may have ideas as to why it happened, perhaps Gill had a previous disagreement with Fred in class, or maybe the two of them never seem to get on. This should be recorded in the relevant area on the incident report. An idea to help prevent this kind of incident happening again may be that Gill and Fred no longer play together, or that they have mediation to try to help resolve the issue. This could be during a Behaviour Management session, perhaps playing a board game or an outdoor game together, with the staff member present, pointing out the good things that are happening between them, however small those things might be.

Pupil views

After a child has had an incident or big issue where staff have needed to intervene, then it can be a good idea to get into the practice of taking pupil views. Often this is best done by someone not directly involved with the incident as the child may still be cross with the member of staff who was involved or is dealing with the incident.

Often a child with AS can have a very logical reason for her actions. It may just be panic and she may not know what else to do. In that case, strategies could be useful. It may be that she merely misunderstood what was happening. It could be that other children are not confident enough to tell the child that she is too rough and they don't like it so the child with AS therefore continues to behave in that way, unaware that she is upsetting people until it is too late.

By taking pupil views, we gain an insight into the way these children view the world. It can be quite logical and we need to be able to understand them. Recording pupil views is a good way of doing that and then helping them to help themselves. It is also a good way for us to view our own practice and see how we can help a child with AS more by the way we do, or say, things.

It is important that, when taking pupil views, it is just that, and not an interpretation of what *you* think happened or what *you* think the child may be saying. If she uses a swear word, then write it down. It could be really relevant. If the child says 'Charlie called me a bastard' don't write: 'She said the child swore at him.' It is important that you record *exactly* what is said because the wording is relevant. It could be Charlie calling her a 'bastard' was the key word that was the antecedent to the incident. That particular word may be a trigger for the child, for one reason or another, and once that is known, it is easier to try to defuse problems in the future.

If the views merely state that she was sworn at it could be misinterpreted and other staff could imagine all sorts of things that could have been said but they are actually none the wiser to finding out what the reasons were for the child to react in the way she did. It's a bit like gossip, you're not quite sure exactly what was said so you fill in the gaps with your own interpretation and get the truth completely wrong. Take a look at the two examples below and see how differently a statement can be interpreted.

PUPIL VIEWS 1   CHILD: GILL ANSELL

Gill said she was in the classroom and the teacher had asked them to get their maths workbooks out and this had upset her as Gill had wanted to do English and then she lost self-control.

PUPIL VIEWS 2   CHILD: GILL ANSELL

I was sat in class and Mrs Hallett told us to get our maths books out. Well, I wasn't having that because we were supposed to have English and Miss Scott had told us yesterday that we could carry on writing our stories first thing in English today. We weren't meant to be doing maths so I carried on and got my English book out and started the next part of my story and Mrs Hallett told me to put it away and when I said 'no' she started shouting at me so I threw the books across the room and left the classroom and slammed the door on my way out. It's all her fault and she shouldn't be there anyway and she's an old bat.

The first statement is clearly an interpretation by the adult as it has been written in the third person, and is a brief version of what Gill had said; it is not what the child had actually stated and is therefore not their views. If another person was reading that statement and trying to discover what led to the incident, it would be very difficult to glean any real information from it.

However, the second statement is written in the first person and it contains a lot more information, such as the following:

- Gill was sure they should not be having maths – why was this?

- Gill had been told by another teacher that she should be having English – why was this?

- Gill said that Mrs Hallett had shouted at her – why did Mrs Hallett do this and was it a regular occurrence?

- Gill has identified that she threw the books across the room and left the classroom and slammed the door – Gill is being honest about her behaviour so it is very likely that she is telling the truth about the rest of the incident.

- Gill said that Mrs Hallett shouldn't be there anyway – why did she think that?

- Gill clearly does not like Mrs Hallett on this occasion – is this a normal reaction for her toward this member of staff?

Before writing the child's statement as in 'Pupil views 2' above, I would make it very clear to the child that I wanted her to tell me *exactly* how things happened and that I was not going to tell her she was right or wrong, that I needed to be clear about what happened and I would only write exactly what she told me. This tells the child that she is being listened to and that what she has to say is important. After taking a statement, I would re-read it to the child to see if she agrees this is what she said.

By looking carefully at the information in Gill's statement, we can see that there are a number of things that have been highlighted. On further investigation it is found that Gill's usual teacher Miss Scott, who had actually told her the day before that they could continue with their English during first period, had phoned in sick that morning. A supply teacher, Mrs Hallett, had been used to cover Gill's class that morning. Gill does not like change anyway and has never been good at accepting supply staff as she does not know them and therefore feels anxious because they in turn do not know her, or about her condition. Gill had not been given any warning that Miss Scott would not be in and therefore had no time to prepare for the changes that morning. Gill has had Mrs Hallett for cover lessons before and Mrs Hallett had not been pre-warned about Gill's behaviour or her AS on her first time at the school so they had a very poor relationship from the start, sometimes leading to Mrs Hallett raising her voice to Gill.

Having read both statements and seen the difference, it is possible to see where Gill's anxieties arose and get a better understanding of why she behaved the way she did. Therefore, it would be easier to prevent such an incident happening again with a little forethought from staff. Next time, Gill could be taken aside and told about the changes to the staff that morning, and the changes to the lesson. Also, it highlights that Gill and Mrs Hallett have a negative relationship and maybe something could be done about that. For example, maybe Gill could tell Mrs Hallett about some of the things she has been doing in Behaviour Management to help her to understand her own behaviour, and to understand that changes do happen, and maybe Mrs Hallett could apologise for shouting at Gill and explain that she had not understood why she was so anxious. I understand that all these things take up time, but again, we are working in schools because we want to help children, and by doing these little things, we could be helping a child in a big way. After all, *every* child matters.

Antecedents

Sometimes there appears to be no reason for the incident. On talking to the child later, when she is calm, it may be possible for you to understand the incident better and note little changes to her behaviour prior to the incident. She may have broken a pencil lead, or her fountain pen ran out of ink, and this could have just been the final thing for her that resulted in her lack of control. These are not necessarily things we would normally notice in a child as, to the majority of children, a broken pencil lead or empty fountain pen is just one of those annoying things that happens sometimes. However, for the child with AS, it could be one of a catalogue of little things that have upset her throughout the morning or day and she might feel that she really can't deal with any more.

Just imagine this: the child is a few minutes late getting up and then has to rush her breakfast. Her sibling is also upset at having to rush and the siblings have a disagreement. The parent then gets upset with them but manages to calm them both before school and they arrive early enough for the start of school. Then, on arrival in class, the child realises she has forgotten her handwriting pen, but manages to write with a pen borrowed from the pencil pot on the table. Then, later, the class move to another room for their next lesson but the child does not take the pen with her and there is not a spare one in the pot on the table now. The teacher asks the children to get on with their work while she sorts out the overhead projector, which is making a clicking noise. The overhead light is also flickering and another child is chatting to you about the work he is doing. The first thing you notice to show that something is wrong is when the child throws the book across the room and starts shouting about how the work is rubbish. However, for the child, this is not the start of the incident – it is merely the final thing in a list of factors that have not gone right that day and she has been unable to communicate that to you.

When talking to a child after an incident, try not to get answers before she is really calm. This could lead to the behaviour escalating again. It may be several hours or even the next day, before you get to talk to her about it. Then all you can do is learn from the incident and try to look out for the antecedents the next time to help prevent a similar incident.

Children need to know that once an incident is over and finished it is not going to be brought up again in a negative way. For example: 'You did this last month and you ended up getting yourself into trouble over it.' This will only help them to feel negative about themselves and make them feel they are not progressing. I have brought up previous incidents when a child has had another similar incident but dealt with it in another way, but would only ever do this when the child is calm and open to talking to me. For example: 'Do you remember when you had a problem like this before and you didn't know how to deal with it? Well, this problem was like that but you have learned to deal with it much better so well done. You are doing really well at learning to manage your own behaviour.' She may not have noticed anything positive in the fact she has had another incident, but pointing out that she has done something right in spite of it can only help her fragile self-esteem. Try not to take incidents personally and remember, it is not the child's fault, it is the way her brain is programmed and we *can* help her to learn strategies to cope with such issues. In turn, she can help us to understand AS a little better, so enriching our lives.

Chapter 25

Graphs

From the details entered on the incident reports it is fairly easy to make graphs, which highlight certain problem areas all at once. For example, using a computer spreadsheet, enter the days of the week that each of the incidents happened over a period of time, for example a half-term. This can help to see the incident data clearly, whereas you may just remember the one that involved you getting a book thrown at you. A graph will clearly show which days have more incidents and which have less (see Figure 25.1). Using this information you may be able to highlight certain factors such as that the incidents mainly happen on Tuesdays and Thursdays which happen to be the days the child goes to after-school clubs. This *could* be a reason for the incidents and could be brought up in parent/teacher meetings. Perhaps the child gets really excited about going or perhaps he hates going but it could give you an insight as to why the child behaves the way he does. It may also be easier to notice an antecedent during those days. The parents may know of another reason for the behaviours on certain days – perhaps it is the child's sibling's turn to choose what to watch on TV after school, or maybe there are no computer games allowed on certain days. By working together with parents, we can achieve so much more for the child.

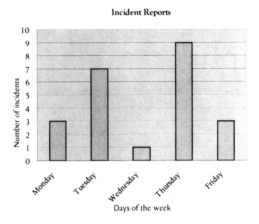

Figure 25.1 Incident data spreadsheet: Example 1

Remember, you are learning, along with the child, about how to help him to help himself. If you can intervene in a positive way before things go wrong, then the child will have learned another strategy to cope with a certain situation.

Graphs can also help you determine what behaviours are most common during incidents (see Figure 25.2).

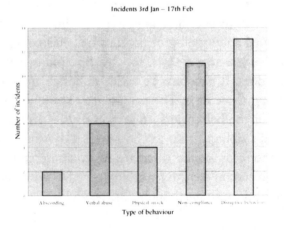

Figure 25.2 Incident data spreadsheet: Example 2

It is clear from the graph in Figure 25.2 that the child's behaviour is very disruptive. It may be that, although the above graph makes it look like there are 36 incidents, there may have been only 13 (although that is still a large amount!) because some incidents may have involved more than one type of behaviour. For example, the child may have refused to do his work (non-compliance) then thrown his pencil case, which hit someone else (disruptive behaviour) and then sworn at someone (verbal abuse) as he ran to get outside and down the school drive (absconding). By showing the incidents in graph form it is easier to see which behaviour needs to be worked on first.

It may seem to you that the child has incidents randomly, but on inspection of the graphs, you may be able to notice trouble spots. For example, he may have most incidents during particular lessons, or at unstructured times of the day. If this is the case, try to work out why they are happening and find ways to help overcome that. It could be that the incidents happen mainly in English classes – and the reason could be easily sorted by, for example, sitting him near to the door so he can go to his time-out area, or ensuring that he understands exactly what the task is – don't forget, just because he may be verbally well spoken, it doesn't always mean he understands vocabulary as well as you think they might. If it shows up on the graphs that the times he has most incidents are during unstructured sessions, for example playtimes and lunchtimes, try to think of strategies to help him – a circle of friends could help, or a separate play area where he feels less threatened by everyone else's noise, etc.

When I have created graphs, I have collated the data every half-term and have used four each time. These are:

1. Days of the week.

2. Type of behaviour.

3. Activity/lesson.

4. Morning or afternoon (I always do this as a pie chart).

Over a period of a school year, the graphs can be a useful tool for showing progress (or not as the case may be) in behaviour. Graphs are also a good tool for showing in reviews. The child may like to see what progress he has made and the graphs can help him understand a bit more about his behaviours and how often he has outbursts. A child I used to work with liked trying to get fewer incidents the following term after reading his graphs for the previous term and I would occasionally remind him how well he was doing as this seemed to help him stay focused. It could be that the child is given a small reward if he is able to have fewer incidents in the forthcoming term. If he does not achieve it, do not make a big thing out of it, merely move on to the next term with a clean slate or make the reward for progress in certain lessons he struggles in so that even if he does not achieve improvement in one subject he can still be rewarded for achieving in another. Any rewards must be achievable by the child and over not too long a time.

Part VI

EVERYTHING ELSE YOU NEED TO KNOW

Chapter 26

Choices and Standing Your Ground

Whereas many of us can make choices from a wide range of things available to us, children with ASD can often find this difficult and if they have too many choices life can become more confusing. Also, these children can have difficulty in understanding language. Therefore, limit the number of choices you give to the child. For example, if a child is having lunchtimes inside for the time being, and you tell her she can do art, or games, or go outside, or play on the computer, or look at a book, she can become overpowered by the number of choices and so many things to try to remember. She then becomes anxious and unsettled as there are too many choices and, because she may like all the activities offered and she is unsure what to choose, it could well lead to unacceptable behaviour. So, it can be better to give her a choice of two things. First of all, you decide what two things can be offered and supported well by yourself or other staff. Then give the child a brief speech.

For example: 'Joanne, you can have the choice of painting or going on the computer this lunchtime. Which would you like to do? Painting or using the computer?'

If the child then decides to choose something different, perhaps going to games club, I have found it better to say that perhaps she could do that another day, but today the choices are painting or time on the computer. By doing this you are enforcing that you are the one giving the choices and that you are prepared to stand by what you have said. This also helps the child to realise that you do what you say you will do and so she gains confidence and trust in you. It will also show the child that you are listening to what she has said if you tell her that you will find out more about her going to games club for another day. You can do this by being firm, but not aggressive, in the way you talk to her.

I was always taught to be firm, fair and friendly and if you can be these three things and consistent as well, you are likely to be someone the child can learn to trust.

Also, be brave enough to have the courage of your convictions. If you believe something could work or should change or be tried, then say so. Just because nobody else is thinking like you, it doesn't mean it can't work or isn't right. I remember sitting in the staff room while a teacher was talking about how (average) students could do this or that for a particular day we had coming up at school. Everyone else sat and agreed with her but I asked how the children with special needs would be involved with it. She replied, somewhat curtly, 'Oh, take your special needs head off for once, Gill.' I was rather embarrassed by her sharpness but knew I had a point so argued it with her, something that is not always easy to do as I am aware that there are schools that do not value their TAs' opinions readily. The outcome was that the aspect of including children with special needs more fully was then considered. The same strategy can be applied to giving instructions to a child. Stand your ground.

Try not to give too many instructions at once. This can become confusing for the child and may cause anxieties to rise because she may not be able to remember all the instructions, then she may forget to do something. This could be seen as a failure on her part and will not help her self-esteem. It may also be a good idea to write the instructions down for her, using bullet points, in which case the child could have more than one or two instructions.

Chapter 27

Bullying

Children with AS, and in fact any child who is different, can be prone to become a victim of bullying behaviour from others, even from adults supposed to be looking out for them. This can obviously lower their already fragile self-esteem.

As part of one of the courses I undertook, I had to carry out a child-related project. I decided to make a bullying awareness video to show the different types of bullying.

Before I started making the video, I surveyed 43 children with AS, individually, and found that *every* one of them had encountered incidents of being bullied. Horrifying to think that *every* child I asked had been bullied.

Sometimes it happened in the streets where they lived, in the many schools they had attended or at clubs they had joined or just at the park. Some even got bullied walking out of their houses onto the street. Usually it seemed to be by small groups as bullies don't often operate on their own. Even if the other children with them are just watching, they are guilty by association.

Since their behaviours are often regarded as 'odd', peers can easily select children with AS as easy prey, and a source of fun for bullies. It is down to us to be particularly vigilant.

Children with AS are renowned for being anxious, and therefore it would not take much to see them react to situations most children would take in their stride. For instance, another child may know that by sitting in the AS child's chair, he can provoke an immediate outburst from the child, which may seem to others to be an exaggerated reaction. If the bully laughs, then so do others – it's the way bullying seems to work.

Therefore, make yourself aware of the school anti-bullying policy and take all bullying seriously. Perhaps your school has, or could have, some kind of programme where children have a place to go if they witness bullying, or are the subject of bullying, or maybe there are specific 'safe' ways for children to report incidents of bullying. Maybe your one-to-one child could help come up with an idea that could be used in your school to help victims of bullying. This could also help build his self-esteem.

Another problem with bullying can be that some children with AS can hold grudges and retaliate, and unless they can see that a situation, or bully in this case, has been properly dealt with, they can feel it is unresolved and therefore try to sort the situation themselves. This isn't just true of children with AS, but remember, children with AS do have difficulty in reading situations, and knowing that things are being done without them actually physically seeing them being done. This is another instance where their trust in staff to deal with things is vital.

Chapter 28

The Translator

As I mentioned on page 31, the English language is complex and one of the first things I learned when I started working with children with AS was that my job, as a special support assistant, was to be a translator. I wasn't quite sure what was meant by that; after all, I only spoke English and my French was limited to 'Bonjour', 'Au revoir' and 'Je m'appelle Gill!' I needn't have panicked, because what this actually meant was that, although the child with AS may be very capable verbally, she may not always understand the meaning of what has been said. I cannot emphasise enough how much misunderstanding language causes distress to children with AS and this is why it is important that we are clear in what we say to these children.

Therefore, when the teacher gives an instruction to the class, check that the child understands what has been asked. Simple words and phrases are not always understood correctly by the child with AS and can often be taken literally. I think this is an area that we, without AS, don't fully appreciate. These are the times that I realise how complicated our language must be to someone with AS and some days I find myself constantly trying to analyse what I say before I say it. I once heard a child explain that having AS was like going to France and not being able to understand anything anyone was saying.

She could see the lips moving and words coming out, but it actually meant nothing at all to her.

It could be that the child has been given the instruction and done exactly what was asked because she may have been unable to understand the unsaid expectations of the teacher, which the other children did understand. Imagine this: a child with AS may have been fidgeting. The teacher then tells her: 'Go to your place and sit there until I tell you to move', then thinks no more about the instruction as the child has gone and sat at her place. The teacher may then explain what the class are doing for that lesson and then tell them to start work. The child with AS may sit there for several minutes before the teacher asks why she isn't doing her work like everyone else, to which the child replies, quite rightly, 'You told me to go to my place and not move until you told me I could. You haven't told me I can move yet.' Exasperating for the teacher, but even more so for the child.

It is not her fault that she understands the world this way, just as it is not our fault that each of us is the way we are. But, we chose the jobs we do, and get paid for doing it, so we need to make *all* lessons accessible for *all* children. If it means that we check the way we talk to children each time we ask them to do things, then so be it. After all, schools *should* be practising differentiation for pupils. This is a small price to pay to help a child fulfil her full potential.

Chapter 29

Finding Solutions

Solutions are things that can be either very hard to find or very simple. It depends on whether it is just you looking for a solution to the problem or whether you have someone with you. I've been quite lucky in that I have usually had other people working quite closely with me and we have been able to bounce ideas off each other and endeavour to find an answer. However, I went to one meeting where we discussed specific difficulties we had with various children and a lady was given umpteen possible solutions to try, but to each she replied, 'We tried that once, it didn't work.' Or 'No, I don't think that would work.' Or 'Yes, it might work but I don't think they'd go for that.'

At times like that I question how much the adult wants to find a solution for the problem. Be positive. There will be a solution out there somewhere, and if the ones that have been suggested don't work or you think they won't, adapt them and keep bouncing ideas off colleagues.

Some common problems and solutions I have tried and that have worked successfully:

- A child is intolerant of noise: remove him from the room to work in another area; use headphones or ear muffs to lessen the noise; use a personal stereo with soft music; give him some time-out.

- A child is fidgety: walk him round the hall a few times or the playground or school field; take him for some skipping or a run around the sports track on the school field; or do some Brain Gym exercises.

- A child wants your attention but is shouting at you: walk away and tell the child, firmly, 'When you are calm, then I will talk to you.' Repeat again after several minutes if the behaviour continues.

- You can see the child is getting anxious in class: use the Space Card and take him out of the room; ask him to write down what the problem is if he does not want to talk to you; or prompt him to use a Referee Card (see Chapter 19 for information about cards).

- A child has problems coming into school each morning: meet him by the front office, allow him to say his quick goodbyes to parents or carers and give him a task, perhaps taking the registers round to all the classes, switching on the computers, and maybe have a colouring activity ready for him, or a puzzle.

- A child does not like the work set: differentiate the work by putting on a picture of, for example, a dinosaur if that is his special interest, or by making the dinosaur part of the lesson by making up questions such as: this dinosaur has 12 spikes on his back, if you colour five blue, how many are left? Put the questions or sums inside a picture of his special interest, such as in a bouncy castle, a monster, or a train. Make the work interesting.

Sometimes just words and numbers on pages isn't enough. (Remember, there are different types of learners, we are not all able to read a whole sheet of work and be inspired.)

- The child gets anxious when he sees the amount of work he is required to do: break it down into smaller chunks and give him part of the work to do first before presenting him with the rest. Maybe give him a few minutes break in between each piece.

- When the child has problems in class and he wants to leave, and doesn't have a direct exit, he may disrupt all the other children: move the child so he always sits near the door so he has an exit available. The same thing applies for attending assemblies, sit him at the end of the row.

- The child does not want to attend assemblies: try to introduce him to assemblies slowly. Sit him on a chair round the corner from the assembly room so he can still hear what is being said but nobody can see him. Then maybe use a sand timer and sit him right at the back, but near an exit, for five minutes and then allow him to leave quietly. Gradually increase the time in the session. You could also use a reward system (see Chapter 19).

- The child plays too roughly: get the children the child is playing too roughly with to tell the child that he is being too rough and that they do not like it. I have had children tell me a child is too rough and I have spoken to him only for him to continue being rough. The child told me 'but they haven't told me it's too rough'. I then got the children to tell the child, with me there, that they did not like the rough play. The child replied 'OK' and then continued playing appropriately. This same idea can be used for other problems where other children are upset by the behaviour of a child with AS.

- Something goes missing and you know or suspect the child with AS has taken it: do not confront him directly, but put the problem in another way. For example, 'I wonder if you can help me, because I've been told that Freddy has lost a pen that was very special to him. Could you help me look for it?' If you take him to the empty classroom or cloakroom and give him some space he may 'find' it and then enjoy the praise for being so helpful.

Chapter 30

Keeping Sane – Seeing the Glass Half Full

After every incident, or problem, no matter how difficult it has been, it can be very easy to get into a negative frame of mind and convince yourself that you are not succeeding in your task. However, if you take a little bit of time actually looking at what has happened that day, it is possible to see something positive. This can be extremely beneficial for your emotional well-being and help you avoid becoming too negative about things, particularly the child.

It may be that the child had a physical outburst that day – which could be deemed negative. But looking at the positive side of things, she may have calmed quicker than she has before, she may have apologised, or she may have gone to her area without prompting. These are just some examples. I have been in weekly meetings about a child where others have only seen 'the glass half empty' and have focused on all the negative aspects of the child's behaviour. Yes, she may have sworn 23 times that afternoon, but the day before she swore 24 times. She may have thrown a chair, which hit you last week, but when she did it this week she missed you. She may not have been in for the music lesson again today, but she did whistle at her bay instead. This is progress and must be seen as such.

However tiny the step may be, it should be celebrated. The child is probably trying really hard for such a small achievement and it should be recognised and she should know that you have recognised it. This is how she will learn that you value everything she achieves and she will respect and trust you for it. It will also help to build her self-esteem. Some of the most rewarding times I have had have been with the children who are more challenging and to just have them say 'Thank you, Miss' one day, makes it all seem worthwhile and as if I have achieved my aim. You could even get yourself a Good Book (see Chapter 22) and put in your achievements on a daily or weekly basis, though remember, only put in positive things. You may have had an horrendous day with a particular child, but she smiled at you when she came into school that morning, so write it down.

It can be very demoralising when you work with a child with challenging behaviour on a one-to-one basis. You can feel very isolated from the rest of the school staff who are talking about lots of children, whereas your focus as a one-to-one worker is limited to just one child. The other children may be doing lots more academic work than your charge, for the time being, and you may feel that you are on your own, but this need not be the case. Believe it or not, you are gaining a lot of knowledge and experience on challenging behaviour because you are dealing with it, and you are also learning more about ASDs and how to help children with them, whereas the other staff are not. You will be gaining a wealth of knowledge that you will one day be able to share with others. Not having the support of someone to talk to about whether or not you have done the right thing with the child that day can also be difficult but it can be remedied. Make a time slot with your teacher, or senior TA, to meet regularly each week, to discuss your concerns, achievements and way forward.

A school I worked in (mainstream) had an educational psychologist (who I must say was extremely supportive, helpful and approachable) who set up termly meetings, during the school day, for TAs and teachers working with ASD children to attend and discuss problems, ideas, resources and sometimes we even had an outside speaker come in to talk to us about autism or AS. These meetings were held alternately in our schools, for a whole morning, and they allowed us to talk about what we sometimes thought of as our failings. We were able to support each other and exchange strategies and thoughts on approaches we had tried or could try. We also exchanged email addresses and telephone numbers so we could give each other support before our next meeting. This also can boost your own self-esteem if you are feeling a bit beaten down by your day but are able to offer advice to a colleague on something you have tried. Especially if they come back to you at a later date and tell you your idea worked with their student.

Or, you could phone your best friend and sound off at them about what a foul day you've had and get it out of your system. It is not healthy to keep all your anxieties in and chatting is a great way to feel better. Others will no doubt give you ideas to try next or tell you what a wonderful job you are doing. It all helps. We could all do with a self-esteem boost sometimes so go for it. Then treat yourself to a glass of wine or a bar of chocolate. You deserve it.

I can remember doing some training with a lady who said that we all get to work with, or are occasionally around, people who irritate us at times. I smiled to myself as I knew exactly what she was talking about. She said that the next time you see this person coming down the corridor towards you, instead of getting uptight, imagine there is a treat (whatever treat you like) perched on top of their head and be pleasant to them. Your reward for being pleasant is whatever you imagined on top of their head. Sounds weird but I thought I would give it a try as I was experiencing feelings of sheer frustration toward a member of staff who I felt was making life difficult for me at work. So, the next time I saw this person walking down the hall towards me, I imagined I saw a chilled glass of chardonnay on their head. I passed the time of day with them and was amazed at how calm I felt. Later that evening I rewarded myself with a glass of chilled white wine and told myself it was all in a day's work and I'd earned it! (I would make a point of not passing this person too many times in the day though or you will probably sleep through the next day! Try a bar of chocolate or a magazine instead sometimes.)

Chapter 31

Jake

- - - - - - - - - - - -

To help others to get a better understanding of what AS is like, I wrote the following poem, entitled 'Jake'. It is not based on any one particular child I have known, but several, and I have used different traits and experiences from various children I have had the pleasure of working with. I also wrote it, originally, for children, but I believe it gives adults a small insight into the life of a child with an ASD. By having this insight, I believe we can understand the condition a little better, and therefore, by understanding it better, we can endeavour to help that child more.

Jake

Jake was not a happy boy, 'cos although he'd really try,
He couldn't understand the world, his parents weren't sure why.
He had a dreadful temper, over things that seemed quite small,
He'd shout and scream and holler, and throw things at the wall.
At the school where Jake had gone, he'd upset all his peers,
He'd failed to make a single friend, which confirmed to him his fears.

He *really* was an alien, that no one understood,
He was alone, on Planet Earth, and that could not be good.
He didn't seem to understand, words other children used,
And then when they explained to him, he just got more confused.
In class they would say silly things, like 'Pull your socks up, Jenny',
But when Jake looked at Jenny's feet, she wasn't wearing any.
So was it Jake that seemed so odd, or were the rest just fuddled,
For things Jake said were clearly fact, but the rest were clearly muddled.
They'd said 'It's raining cats and dogs', so Jake looked out the window,
'There *are* no animals out there, it's raining H_2O!'
He also had his set routines, each day they were the same,
If people dared to alter them, then they would get the blame.
For he'd go into a dreadful rage, there's nothing they would gain,
For the routine *had* to happen, and he'd have to start again.
Jake couldn't cope, when things got changed, he thought it most unfair,
Things changing almost every day, was more than he could bear.
A different teacher in the class, was not how it should be,
So Jake would shout and scream and cry, for all his peers to see.

Perhaps he *was* an alien, who was sent to change some things,

To sort Earth's funny language, and the problems that it brings.

The other children teased him, they called him weird, and freak,

'Who'd want to hang around with you? You're nothing but a geek.'

Jake found life frustrating, and took comfort in his toys,

He'd line up all his dinosaurs, but not like earthling boys.

They had a certain order, it's the way they had to be,

Triceratops, Pteranadon, and big fierce Rex, were always one, two, three.

He had over a hundred, of these prehistoric things,

If anyone upset his lines, then chaos it would bring.

He'd go into a panic, hit out at who was near,

Just why Jake couldn't cope with this, would soon become quite clear.

Mum took him to the doctor, who sent him for some tests,

To find out what the problem was, they'd started on a quest.

But then he saw a doctor, who wore glasses made of chrome,

You're not an alien, young Jake, you've Asperger's Syndrome.

He then went on to say, that it's quite a common fate,

And just because you have it, doesn't mean you can't be great.

Just look at Albert Einstein, they think he had it too,

He tested science theories, and found them to be true.

When Jake heard what the doctor said, it made things much more clear,

Jake now understood much more, it helped to quell his fear.

So Jake was not an alien, he was filled now with relief,

He was pleased the doctor talked to him, and quashed his daft belief.

It was a common factor, that for someone with AS,

They always liked to deal with facts, they didn't like to guess.

And Jake was also pleased, that there were others just like him,

That some excelled in certain things, it need not be too grim.

So Mum talked to the teachers, and some strategies were made,

To help Jake fit in at school, some ground rules now were laid.

Each day he'd have these sessions, to help Jake understand,

About AS and friends and rules, and help was now at hand.

Now Jake could choose a different child, to spend time with every day,

And instead of having tantrums, he'd be shown a different way.

He learned to talk about the things, that made young Jake see red,

He was shown some other things to do, good things to try instead.

Like squeezing pots of playdough, or
pushing a brick wall,
Or asking for some 'time-out', to calm
down in the hall.
Then, over time, young Jake became,
a much more popular guy,
He found that he could now fit in, so
waved the 'alien' goodbye.

Chapter 32

Learning Curves

The following are little snippets of important things I have learned from my time working with children with ASDs. I hope they will give you an insight into how children with ASDs think and behave and will give you an understanding of how difficult they sometimes find it to communicate and understand our language. It should also show how we need to correct our language and behaviour to help them function better and become more relaxed as they become happier in their knowledge of the world around them. Often we will have to analyse what they are communicating in order to understand what their needs are. We need to remember that these are children who have difficulty in three main areas – the Triad of Impairment – and that if they are doing something we don't understand then it is not because they are necessarily being awkward but because it is the only way they know, at present, to communicate their wants, needs or feelings. It is up to us to help them find more suitable ways to convey their message.

> *I remember working with a child with AS on a practice test paper. The question was something like this: if the candle burns one inch in two hours, how much will it have burned after six hours? To me the answer was simple, three inches.*

> *But to this child, who was very bright, it*
> *was troubling him because the question*
> *didn't say exactly how long* after *six hours*
> *the candle burned, therefore he could not*
> *possibly answer the question. He spent*
> *a long time looking at the question and*
> *refused to move on for ages until I sug-*
> *gested he return to it later. The reason for*
> *his concern for this question had me puz-*
> *zled. He left the answer blank.*

It is situations like this where I have learned how difficult things must be for some children. We tend to forget that language is something they find difficult and I am constantly being reminded of this when they have outbursts or become withdrawn. In this case, he remained calm but studied the question for a long time, losing valuable time in a test. Sometimes, just re-wording what we say can be of enormous benefit to a child. This is also helpful for children with AS who are academically able. When a child has the instruction, ask him what it means just to clarify he knows exactly what has been said.

> *A child I was working with was asked if*
> *he could describe what it was like to have*
> *AS. He said that he felt a bit like how*
> *a fish might feel if the rest of his shoal*
> *of fish were swimming in the other direc-*
> *tion.*

I think this gives a good description of how he must have felt, that everyone else was working towards the same thing, but he seemed unable to do so because he had AS, and that he was very different from everyone else, more so when he was in a mainstream setting. At first this child was angry because he had AS and was different from his peers but gradually he became happier with who he was and felt that having AS was actually an advantage because without it he wouldn't be him. A big step forward in this process was when he learned that the creator of Microsoft, Bill Gates, might well have AS and if Mr Gates could achieve all he had with AS then there was nothing to stop him achieving what he wanted to do.

> *Although children with AS may be very articulate in their language skills, their understanding is not always as advanced and therefore their vulnerability not always recognised. When I was talking to a 15-year-old about him being able to go into town on his own for the first time, he said to me: 'My mum says I have to be aware of strangers. Miss, how will I know if someone's a stranger?'*

This question was asked of me from a boy who had regularly watched violent and sexual video films at home (rating certificates were well above his age and understanding), yet here he was, extremely vulnerable in that he did not know how to tell if someone was a stranger. I told him that if he didn't know the person then they were a stranger. This information shocked him and he became much more aware of the number of strangers he would encounter in town when he went in alone or with peers.

> *Sex education lessons are always sessions I don't look forward to with children with AS. During such a lesson with teenagers, the subject was about women and menstruation. One 15-year-old then told us: 'But my mum doesn't have periods and she certainly doesn't use those things [tampons] because if she did, she'd have*

told me about it and I haven't seen any of
them about our house. Besides, it's gross.'

It may sound funny, because we understand about these things, but because this child's mother kept her tampons out of sight, and because he hadn't seen them, then to him, it couldn't possibly be true that his mother had periods. Even when staff carefully explained to him that women have periods in order for them to have children, he was not convinced. The whole idea disgusted him and because he loved his mother, he believed that she could not possibly be subjected to anything so gross. In cases like this, it can take a while for the child to learn about the lesson being taught. Their learning may not necessarily be instant or in one or two lessons.

Many of us have Asperger traits if we
are honest. For example, I used to park
in the staff car park where there were
about 80 spaces. When I arrived at work,
there would only be about seven cars in
the car park and I would always reverse
park in the same space. That was, until
a new maintenance man started work
and I went into work one morning to
find he had parked in my *space! The fact*
that there were about 73 other spaces
available for me made no difference to
the fact that I felt unsettled. A colleague
had also noticed that I had had to park
in another space that morning and joked
that she thought I must be very edgy with
my unplanned situation that morning,
and that perhaps I had AS. But then,
when she and I went into the staff room
for coffee later that day she said, quite

seriously, 'Oh, blast! Anne's sat in my
seat.' I couldn't help but laugh.

Next time you go into the staff room for coffee break, look to see who has a regular seating place, and looks perplexed when someone else is in it. If nobody else usually sits in it, it could be interesting for you to sit in it to test out this theory (if of course, you're brave enough and provided it's not the boss'). The same can be applied to the car park.

For me, I like to write children's stories in verse but *have* to write 32 verses. My stories are not complete until I have that magic number and I would not consider it completed until that thirty-second verse is done. Some friends of mine, not diagnosed with AS, count the syllables in road names and for them this is a habit, similar to some of the traits in children and adults with AS. A few people I have worked with like to smell the paper in new books or packs of paper. It doesn't mean that everyone around us has undiagnosed AS, but merely that many of us have funny little habits that make up who we are, the same as for these children with AS. It is worth bearing this in mind when you think the child you are working with is behaving strangely. We all do it (and those who say they don't are lying!).

A child I had been working with had been particularly rude to me and was asked, by the teacher, to write me a letter of apology. An hour or so later I was handed an envelope by the child. I opened the envelope and read his very nice apology. It was only when I turned the letter over that I noticed he'd drawn a picture of me on the back of it – dressed as a witch! I

> *thanked him and told him I accepted his*
> *apology and the day continued as usual.*

Knowing when to challenge a child, and when not to, is something that is learned over time, when you know the child well. This was a relatively new child to us. We could have challenged the child over the picture he'd drawn, but the fact was he'd apologised and he had compromised. We, as the responsible adult, do not always have to challenge everything – he had done what was asked of him and he had made his little protest but the day continued with little more disruption. If we had challenged him again, the day could have resulted in a more disruptive incident.

> *Always try to keep track of what you are*
> *saying to a child who has AS. I once kept*
> *a child back after a lesson to discuss the*
> *meaning of his poor behaviour. I started*
> *by asking him a question about his be-*
> *haviour, but each time I said something,*
> *he asked me to clarify what I was asking.*
> *After several minutes of this conversation*
> *he had managed to confuse me so much*
> *I couldn't remember what I had initially*
> *asked him! He then went out to break*
> *with a big smile whilst I sat there won-*
> *dering how on earth I had got myself into*
> *that mess.*

When challenging a child, keep things simple – ask one question and wait for the response. Clarify your question if need be but try to remain the one in control of the conversation and don't allow him to divert you from the question you want answered.

We had noticed a child's behaviour change for the worse over a couple of days but, when asked, he always said he was fine. Having no other explanation for the child's behaviour, we took him to the school doctor who promptly diagnosed an ear infection. After starting antibiotics, the child's behaviour returned to how it usually was.

Children with ASDs are not always able to express their discomfort appropriately when they are feeling unwell due to having a high pain threshold. This particular child had been tearful and grumpy and quite disruptive in class for a couple of days, which was not typical behaviour for him. He was unable to tell us his ear hurt and, having no other explanation for his poor behaviour, it was up to us to make the decision for him to go to the doctors. Fortunately, we did it in time for the ear infection to clear up before becoming worse. A similar scenario occurred when a child complained when his arm hurt after he had it hit by a football on the playground. He was taken to casualty and the X-rays showed it had been broken before but his parents and school had no record of it being broken previously.

Sometimes children are more in control than we might give them credit for. After being hit several times by a child, I told the child that he could not behave that way in public. He replied, 'Oh, I wouldn't do that in public, you're staff, so it doesn't matter.' It came as quite a shock to him when I explained that I was a member of the public, who just happened to work in school!

Only when you know a child well are you able to tell whether they are behaving negatively due to his AS or just because he is being like any other child and being naughty. Often, you are able to see an element of control when he is displaying negative behaviour. For example, if he is throwing things around the room, but leaves the things that he likes alone, such as his belongings or the computer he likes to use, then there is some control there. A child has completely lost control when these things are not considered during an aggressive outburst and he is unable to consider the consequence of his actions or hear any choices you may give him. A child I worked with was about to kick me until I reminded him that the last time he did I had to see the doctor. He then walked away, showing an element of control and being able to understand the consequence of what he was about to do.

> *Whilst marking a child's maths questions I noticed that the answers he had given were out by several thousand each time. When I asked how he had got to the answers he had, he said, 'The book says to "write your answer", so I did.' He had not understood that he had to work out the sum and not just write any number he thought of.*

This was a case of the way the question had been written in the maths text book. The child had read the question but it had not said he had to work out the answer. After the teacher explained this to him, he was able to complete the questions with the correct answer. This was a child who was very literal in his thinking. Other children with AS had used the same textbook but had understood that they needed to work out the sum beforehand. Remember, each child is different and just because one child with AS understands something then it does not necessarily mean the next one will understand or interpret something the same. It is not because he is being awkward, his way of thinking is just different.

> *One weekend, I was having Christmas drinks with my children and siblings and their families in a local pub. A 15-year-old, with AS, that I worked with, walked into the same pub and sat down next to me, and members of my family. I said hello, and told him I was having drinks with family. He asked if I would buy him a drink. I had to explain to him that as I was with family, it would not be appropriate for him to join us. 'Oh,' he replied looking surprised and not really understanding what was expected of him, 'Should I go then?'*

Although this was a family gathering, and he had not been invited, the child thought it was OK to just sit down and stay with me. There was no embarrassment on his part. He had missed all social cues that it was not the thing to do to just sit and join me. Back at school I explained to him that it was OK for us to say hello in the street if we met, but that I was his TA and that socialising together outside of school was not appropriate. He had his friends for that. Once he understood this, he was happy about what had happened.

> *A child I worked with had a special interest in films of a violent nature. As he was only 14, we tried to divert his obsessive talk about such films with other ideas. So, every time he started talking about*

these films, I would talk over him about Disney films and tell him how exciting they were. I emphasised how I really liked The Little Mermaid *film. He would just shrug his shoulders and stop talking, for a while. Then, one day, he was asking if I had seen the latest action film, where just about everyone gets blown to smithereens and every other woman gets raped until the hero saves them. I interrupted him and started talking about* The Little Mermaid *and said how nice it was and about the bad old octopus. Having used this strategy with him for several weeks, he looked me in the eye and, very seriously, said 'Miss, I think you have a problem. You're obsessed with Disney films.'*

We had told this boy many times we were not interested in his obsession but he would state 'Yes but ...' and continue to tell us about the bits in the particular film he found exciting. Gradually, this boy came to realise that not everyone was interested in the same things as him. Sometimes I would interrupt a child's obsessive talk by talking about how I made a cake at the weekend, stating every detail from weighing the flour to the shape of tin I used. When they asked why I kept talking about boring stuff, I would answer that I found their talk of computer games or violent films boring, but that I liked baking cakes and talking about them. Only then did the child start to realise that not everyone was interested in his, or other people's, obsessions and his talking about it constantly.

Building a positive working relationship with trust goes both ways. I once worked with a child who had a pet hamster and, after giving him several targets to help him achieve certain things, he decided to give me my own target. Knowing I was terrified of rodents (and seeing me jump on a chair when his escaped from its cage one morning) he decided that I had to try and hold his hamster for five seconds. First, I had to just stroke the hamster and after about a week, he decided I had to put it in my hand and he would time me. Not wanting to look like a complete wimp, I stood there bravely holding this hamster in my hand for what felt like an eternity, before losing my self-control and screaming like a baby for him to 'Quick! Take it back, Quick!' This taught me a very important lesson. Just because we find some things easy to do, don't assume other people do.

It took me weeks and weeks to be able to hold this hamster and it could be the same for a child to overcome his reluctance to be able to do something. One child I know would disrupt every music lesson he was in and it was thought it was because he wanted to use one instrument and to do his own thing, rather than work as part of the group. It turned out it was because he was noise sensitive and could not cope with 30 or so other children in the room banging and playing all the instruments together and it not having the structure of a melody. For several weeks he would just spend five minutes in each music lesson (watching an egg timer) and would sit outside the classroom for the rest of the lesson, with the door closed to begin with. Slowly, he was able to build up time in the lessons until he was able to function appropriately in the music lesson for the whole amount of time. Surely, it is better to achieve over a longer period of time than to not achieve at all by forcing the child to comply with the normal routines.

> *Try to find fun ways to encourage a child to get their task completed. One child I worked with had heard me sing in their music lessons and in assemblies and always winced when I sang. When I was taking him for a one-to-one computer session, where he was using a daily 15-minute spelling programme, he started to get up and walk away from the computer. I cleared my throat and told him I would have to sing to him then. He looked absolutely panic-stricken and, returning promptly to his seat and the task, he said 'No, Miss, anything but that'. This strategy worked every time, and he even used to test me enough for me to have to sing a few bars before he settled to his work and informed me he was doing it!*

This child used to tell his peers to get on with work or I would sing to them. It was a fun way to get the task done (and I'm sure my singing isn't really that bad). I used the same tactic when he was constantly walking or running around with his hands in his pockets. I would clear my throat ready to start singing to him but before I could release the first note he would have his hands out of his pockets and be walking properly with a smile on his face. His peers would even warn him that I would sing to him if he didn't act quickly!

After practising, for several weeks, how to behave in a café, we then tried to put it all into practice by visiting a local café with the children. We told each child they had £2.00 to spend. After queuing for several minutes and talking to the assistant behind the counter, one child returned to us but had bought nothing. When asked why, he replied 'Because I have £2.00 and there is nothing there that costs £2.00'. We hadn't explained that all the cakes and drinks were less than £2.00 and that he could get one of each and that he would be given change. He'd assumed he had to spend exactly £2.00.

It is only by witnessing these types of behaviours that we can fully begin to appreciate how disabling having a literal mind can be in our society. However, we learned a lot about this child by doing this task. We had to check that he fully understood what he could or couldn't do in certain situations and we were better able to prepare him for such events in the future. During lessons, we had to explain things more clearly and in more detail than we normally do and we had to be aware of every part of the language we used. For these children, our language is already confusing, so using any of the following types of statements will be futile:

- Pull your socks up (for what reason?)

- Keep your hair on (will it fall off if they don't?)

- Hold your horses (do they have any?)

- Play it by ear (is that actually possible?)

- A fate worse than death (what is worse than death?)

These are statements we use frequently, without realising, but they can cause a lot of worry to a literal child so try not to use them or explain what they mean when you do use them. I often ask 'Have you heard the saying…' and then explain what it means, because they may well hear it again from someone else but at least they will then have the understanding of what we mean when saying it.

> *I asked a child to explain, in his own words, what AS was like. After some thought he said. 'It's a bit like a plastic ruler, it can bend a little but if you bend it too far it will snap.'*

This gives a very good insight in to how a child with AS feels and explains about his rigidity in some areas (inflexibility of thought). When the child told me this I clarified what he meant by asking him 'So, when we try to show you different methods of doing your maths, when you already know a method, this makes you feel angry and can cause you to be disruptive?' He replied 'Yes'. It took a long time and a lot of patience to show him how to do various mathematical problems in different ways, but we accepted that if he would calmly try them a few times, we assured him he could always return to his preferred method. With this security available to him, he tried other methods and even found some of them quicker and easier to use than the methods he already knew.

> *One 15-year-old boy with AS once told me that he was going to kill my children when he was older and then kill me. Later, that same day, he offered me some of his chocolate. I refused and told him I was still upset about what he had said earlier, and he told me, with all sincerity,*

that he wouldn't really do that, he had just said it because he was angry about his schoolwork. He then apologised and re-offered the chocolate. It was the only time he ever said he would harm my family – he just swore at me thereafter!

Try not to take insults personally as the child doesn't usually mean it – he is just angry for a short amount of time and has not yet learned other acceptable strategies to deal with this anger. It is up to us to show him other ways, but not during an incident, only when he is calm. Showing him when he is angry is futile as his brain is not accepting messages he can interpret. Wait until he is fully calm, which may be the next day or several days later, when he is able to talk about what happened and how he could deal with it better if the same thing, or a similar thing, happened again.

Whilst sitting in his bay, helping him with his maths, I noticed the 14-year-old kept looking at me and smiling. I asked what he was smiling at. He replied, 'You're sat in my bay because you fancy me, don't you miss?' Needless to say, I told him very firmly that I did not fancy him at all and left him to do his maths alone!

A short while later, I was able to talk with this boy and explain that I was merely there to help him and that there was no way that any of the staff would be employed if it was thought they would behave inappropriately with the children. I also explained that to help him with his work, staff would need to sit with him, but that it did not mean that staff fancied him, or any other boy. After this explanation, he understood and I never had any problems with him regarding this matter again.

> *I have found that using acronyms with some children is a fun, and discreet, way to work with them when they are having problems and to remind them that their behaviour needs adjusting without bringing it to their peers' attention too much (see Chapter 12). I used 'Double O' for 'Opting Out' and 'PTB' for 'Pushing The Boundaries' for example. One child liked us using acronyms as his peers were really keen to know what the codes meant but we wouldn't explain them to them. In a mainstream class with about 34 students, the student I worked one to one with was reluctant to start his work, preferring to chat and joke with peers instead. So I asked him to get on with his handwriting and that we didn't want a 'Double O day' or a 'PTB' day today. He smiled and said, 'No, I think it's a KMA day.' I looked at him, puzzled as this was a new one for me, and asked 'What's that?' to which he replied, tongue in cheek, 'A Kill Miss Ansell day!' Just as well I understood his humour!*

Humour is a wonderful thing but it needs to be used with care. Some children with AS do not understand humour and think you are laughing at them. Once again, it is about knowing your student. Some students I have worked with understand and like sarcasm, but many do not. Humour can be a great way to turn a child's negative behaviour around by using it as a distraction. One of the students found out I had injured my leg hopping over a gate and asked how I could have been in the army if I was so unfit I couldn't jump over a gate. I told him it was because I was a double agent and needed to infiltrate the hospital so had to pay a price for my job so as not to alert the hospital staff to who I was. This joke became very popular with a couple of the students. When one of them was having an incident where he had thrown his chair across the room, sworn at the teacher and walked out of class swearing some more, I followed him. He stood by a tree and was clearly very angry and was swearing at me, though not about me. I interrupted him as I touched my ear, as if I had an imaginary earpiece, and said, 'Hang on a minute, I'm getting a message from Barack (Obama) about my next mission.' The boy laughed and started talking about whether it would involve a helicopter or jumping over more gates to infiltrate more hospitals. After we chatted about nonsense for a few minutes, and he calmed down, I asked him what the problem had been in class; he was able to tell me and we were able to sort the problem quite quickly.

I used to use a hedgehog glove puppet with some of the younger students. I used to pretend that the hedgehog, Hovis, whispered in my ear about how the students were doing with their work. One particular boy had seen me putting the glove puppet in my drawer at the end of each lesson, and therefore, I assumed he realised it was not real. I had also pretended that Hovis visited the boy's real guinea pig which was kept in a nearby shed. However, I came into work one morning to find that he had been up quite early as he had set a trap by his

> *pet's shed because he thought Hovis was*
> *stealing his guinea pig's food!*

Never assume! I had believed, falsely as it turned out, that this child knew the puppet was not real as he had seen me put it on my hand after taking it from the drawer, and later removing it from my hand and placing it back in the drawer after the lesson. He had believed me when I had said that Hovis had eaten some of his guinea pig's food, even though the puppet was clearly not real. The boy, although aged about nine, had a low level of understanding and I had not fully appreciated it.

> *I once worked with a child who had all*
> *the classic symptoms of AS but because*
> *his aunt had told him there was no such*
> *condition, he firmly believed it did not*
> *exist and so therefore, he thought, he*
> *couldn't possibly have something that did*
> *not exist. I don't think I actually helped*
> *this child in any way and I feel that, al-*
> *though he was entitled to believe what he*
> *wanted, it didn't actually serve him well.*
> *Therefore, I don't feel that I failed in this*
> *instance. Sometimes, our best will never*
> *be good enough because some people re-*
> *sist the help we offer and so maybe we*
> *should therefore concentrate on those we*
> *can help and who want to be helped.*

However, if I knew then what I know now, then maybe I could have done some work with him about the syndrome and maybe, just maybe…

> *I once asked a young boy with AS how he*
> *felt about having AS. He replied, 'I like*
> *it, because if I didn't have it I wouldn't*

think the way I think and I wouldn't be me.'

Having AS doesn't have to be a negative thing, as this young man had decided. On the computer, if you 'Google' search 'famous people with AS' it will bring up pages of famous people who have, or are thought to have, AS. Without it they would probably not have been as successful in their chosen profession. I have used these pages to show people with AS how it can be a positive thing – too often they believe that because they have this condition they will never achieve anything positive which is totally untrue.

Sometimes the behaviours can be quite complex. At a boarding school for special needs, a 14-year-old came into class one morning with a black eye. We asked how he had got it (having seen him the day before without it, and not hearing anything about it that morning in the daily briefing) and he told us he had fallen in his room the night before. Not quite understanding what had happened and wondering why the care staff had not picked up on this at breakfast, I went across to the care staff at morning break and asked. They seemed as mystified as us, stating that he had not had it at breakfast. The care member then knocked on the door and went into his room (the door was open) to witness the young man expertly applying pink and blue make-up around his eye!

After careful questioning by staff of the student, it turned out that the student had wanted to get someone to notice that he wanted to talk to them but he was unable to express this verbally.

> *Children with AS can be quite blunt about things, not always understanding social etiquette. One 14-year-old I met when I first started work in a special school, asked me, in front of the rest of the class, if I had any children. I replied, 'Yes, I have two.' To which he replied, 'So you've had sex twice then?'*

I did not answer his question – I conveniently took it as a rhetorical question. This child was certainly unaware that it is possible to have sex for more than the single reason of having a baby.

> *Noticing a 16-year-old I used to work with, out of class, I went to ask him what was wrong. He told me that he had met this girl at the weekend and they had kissed, then she had complained that she had tummy ache. He then went on to say 'that means she's pregnant doesn't it? I know, because I've seen it happen in films.'*

After talking to him at length, and knowing that he had problems distinguishing between fantasy and reality, I realised that he had seen a film where the couple had kissed, and in a few scenes later (probably several months in the film) the woman had been pregnant. This is a typical example of the misunderstandings some children with AS can have.

> *Just when I thought I'd cracked it! Whilst working with a class (seven pupils) of eight and nine-year-olds whilst*

*the teacher was in a meeting, I compli-
mented myself on how well I had settled
the class at their individual bays to do
their English work. It was so quiet you
could have heard a pin drop. Then, the
quietest, most well behaved of the boys,
leaned back on his chair and asked the
others 'Hands up if you think Miss is a
lemon pie?' The others were so surprised
by this question, the whole class erupted
in raucous laughter just as the teacher
walked back in.*

That'll teach me to be so smug! It taught me to remember
that things can change at any moment and to never get
ahead of myself and think I have got things sorted!

*A child I was working with had left the
classroom in a rage over problems with
other children. When I went to the other
building to see if he was calming down,
he ran at me holding a wooden rolling
pin, then stood in front of me threatening to hit me with it. I chose my moment
and put him in a one-person escort (SCIP
hold), allowing him to safely drop the
rolling pin to the ground.*

Immediately I could feel his whole body relax, as if to say
'Thank goodness for that, I'm no longer in control of my
behaviour, you are.' After I walked him to another room,
he calmed down quite quickly. Sometimes, these children
just want someone else to physically take control (in a
recognised way) and make them feel safe again and that
person could be you (as long as you are restraint-trained
of course).

I had driven to work with a colleague one beautiful summer morning, the sun was shining, the birds were singing and there had been a jolly Rolf Harris song on the radio entitled 'It's Gonna Be A Fine Day'. As we got out of the car, I said to my colleague 'I wonder what sort of day we'll have today?' and she smiled sweetly at me. We then entered the garden to the classroom where we worked and hanging out of an upstairs window was a student who shouted at us 'And you two f***ing horse f***ers can f*** off back to where you f***ing came from.'

Quite simply, that was my question answered! In fact, although this is how the day started, the young man in question went on to have a really good day. He'd just had a minor, verbal blip, but with staff support, he managed to turn his behaviour around in a positive way.

I was having a few problems with a teenager I was working with accepting me as his previous class TA had been with him for some time. He was very rude and offhand with me and, as I was quite new to the job and his class, I wasn't quite sure how to handle it. I decided I had two choices: I could either let him walk all over me or I could confront him. I opted for the latter, so when he next refused my assistance I told him, somewhat firmly: 'Look, I don't really care whether you like me or not but Miss V. has gone now and you've got me and I have no intention of going anywhere, so you either deal with it and let me help you with your work or you get on and do it on your own. Your choice.' He looked at me with a rather shocked expression on his face and said 'But I like you Miss, we're friends aren't we? And I could do with some help with my maths.'

From then on he accepted me and was happy for me to help him with his work. He had had difficulty accepting the change that had occurred and he was unsure of the role I played. Explaining it to him was all he needed.

Always treat each child as an individual as every child is different, even every child with an ASD. I remember learning very quickly not to tell a particular child that I would take him to see the head-teacher if he did not get on with his work, after he had sat daydreaming for half the morning and after several requests to get started on his work. Thinking he was the same as all the other children in the ASD school, I told him to get his coat and we would walk over to the head-teacher's office and he could tell her why he was not doing any work. After we had both donned our coats I took him outside where it promptly began raining quite hard. However, forgetting he sometimes had a routine of walking forward three paces, then bending and feeling each of his shoes, walking back a couple of steps, then walking forward three steps, feeling his shoes again, then a couple of steps backwards, etc., it took us (a very drenched us at that!) about 20 minutes to do a three minute walk!

The consequences which may be suitable for the majority of students may not be suitable for all children – they are all individuals and should be treated as such. Needless to say, the next time he didn't start his work I found other ways to encourage him.

And finally:

> *In a primary class, we had been talking about the story of the Good Samaritan in a Religious Education lesson and we then talked about who could help us if we were in trouble, and whom we could ask for help if we needed it. The teacher asked the first child 'Who would you call if you saw a man snatching a handbag from an old lady?' He replied, 'I'd call the police, Miss.' She congratulated him on his answer and then asked the next child 'What would you do if you saw somebody collapse in the street?' He replied 'I'd put him on a donkey, Miss!'*

Here endeth the lesson.

Index

Lightning Source UK Ltd.
Milton Keynes UK
UKOW02f1250111214

242989UK00001B/31/P